Hal Leonard Student Piano Library

Piano Lessons

Book 2

FOREWORD

When music excites our interest and imagination, we eagerly put our hearts into learning it. The music in the **Hal Leonard Student Piano Library** encourages practice, progress, confidence, and best of all – success! Over 1,000 students and teachers in a nationwide test market responded with enthusiasm to the:

- variety of styles and moods
- natural rhythmic flow, singable melodies and lyrics
- "best ever" teacher accompaniments
- improvisations integrated throughout the **Lesson Books**
- orchestrated accompaniments included in audio and MIDI formats.

When new concepts have an immediate application to the music, the effort it takes to learn these skills seems worth it. Test market teachers and students were especially excited about the:

- "realistic" pacing that challenges without overwhelming
- clear and concise presentation of concepts that allows room for a teacher's individual approach
- uncluttered page layout that keeps the focus on the music.

The **Piano Practice Games** books are preparation activities to coordinate technique, concepts, and creativity with the actual music in **Piano Lessons**. In addition, the **Piano Theory Workbook** presents fun writing activities for review, and the **Piano Solos** series reinforces concepts with challenging performance repertoire.

The **Hal Leonard Student Piano Library** is the result of the efforts of many individuals. We extend our gratitude to all the teachers, students and colleagues who shared their energy and creative input. May this method guide your learning as you bring this music to life.

Best wishes,

Barbara Kreader   Fred Kern   Phillip Keveren   Mona Rejino

Authors
**Barbara Kreader, Fred Kern,
Phillip Keveren, Mona Rejino**

Consultants
Tony Caramia, Bruce Berr,
Richard Rejino

*Director,
Educational Keyboard Publications*
Margaret Otwell

Editors
Anne Wester, Rodney Kendall

Illustrator
Fred Bell

To access audio visit:
www.halleonard.com/mylibrary

Enter Code
8772-8397-9752-9826

Book: ISBN 978-0-7935-8439-0
Book/Audio: ISBN 978-0-634-05555-3

HAL•LEONARD®
CORPORATION
7777 W. BLUEMOUND RD. P.O. BOX 13819 MILWAUKEE, WI 53213

Visit Hal Leonard Online at
www.halleonard.com

REVIEW OF BOOK ONE

THE GRAND STAFF

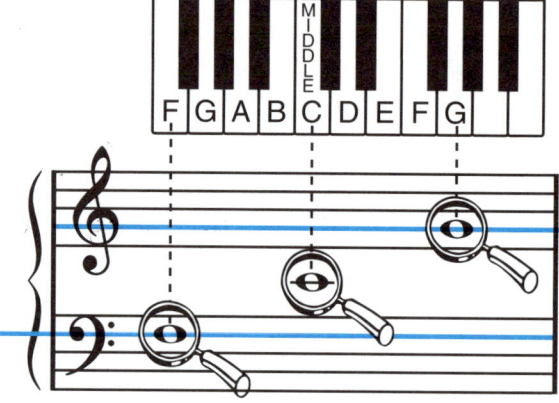

The **G note** is your reading guide for the **Treble or G Clef** (𝄞)

The **F note** is your reading guide for the **Bass or F Clef** (𝄢)

Middle C is your reading guide for the notes between the Treble and Bass Clefs.

NOTE VALUES

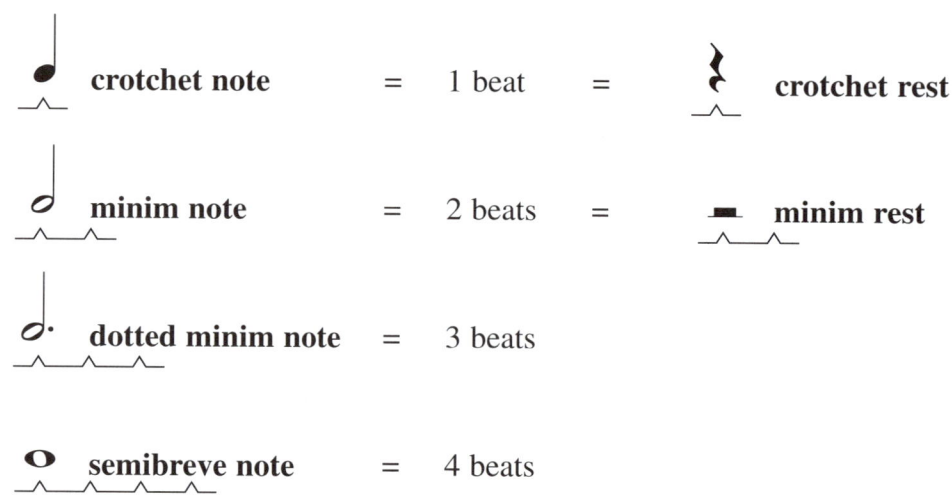

♩ crotchet note	=	1 beat	=	𝄾	crotchet rest
𝅗𝅥 minim note	=	2 beats	=	▬	minim rest
𝅗𝅥. dotted minim note	=	3 beats			
𝅝 semibreve note	=	4 beats			

DYNAMIC SIGNS tell how loudly or softly to play and help create the mood of the music.

p	(piano)	=	soft
mp	(mezzo piano)	=	moderately soft
mf	(mezzo forte)	=	moderately loud
f	(forte)	=	loud

MUSICAL TERMS

time signatures 4/4 3/4

repeat sign 𝄇

D.C. (Da Capo) al Fine means to return to the beginning (capo) and play until you see the sign for the end (fine).

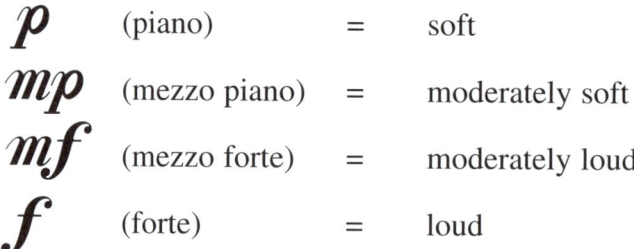

steps

skips

tied notes

TEMPO MARKS tell the mood of the piece and the speed of the pulse.

Adagio	Andante	Allegro
slowly	*walking speed*	*quickly*

CONTENTS

UNIT 1 PLAYING C D E F G

* ✔

		Lesson Book	Games Book	Theory Workbook	Solo Book
Reflection		4		2	
My Own Song	*improvising on C D E F G*	5			
Ode To Joy		6		3	
Carmen's Tune		7	3	4	3
Andantino	*legato* ♩♩♩	8	4	6	4
Big Ben		9		7	
Please, No Bees!	*harmonic intervals, 2nds & 3rds*	10	6	8	
Clapping Song	*staccato* ♩♩♩	11	7	10	6

UNIT 2 4THS

		Lesson Book	Games Book	Theory Workbook	Solo Book
Hoedown	*4ths*	12	8	12	
Sunlight Through The Trees		13	10	13	8
Bingo	*upbeat*	14	13	14	
Travelling Along The Prairie		15	14	15	10
No One To Walk With	< >	16	16		11
Painted Rocking Horse		18	18	16	
Tick Tock The Jazz Clock		20	19	17	

UNIT 3 5THS

		Lesson Book	Games Book	Theory Workbook	Solo Book
Watercolors	*5ths*	22	22	18	
Circle Dance	*two-note slurs* ♩♩	23	24	19	12
Basketball Bounce		24	26	20	
Allegro	*8va*⌐	25		21	
Great News!	*8va*⌐ *ff*	26	28		
Brass Fanfare		27	29		

UNIT 4 SHARPS ♯, FLATS ♭ & NATURALS ♮

		Lesson Book	Games Book	Theory Workbook	Solo Book
Little River Flowing	♯	28		22	
Quiet Thoughts		29	30		14
Star Quest	*A B A form*	30		23	18
A Little Latin	♭	32	32	24	
Stompin'	>	33	34		20
First Light	*ritard*	34		25	22
Inspector Hound	♮	36	36	26	24
Bayou Blues	𝄐	37	37	28	26
Serenade		38			

UNIT 5 PLAYING G A B C D

		Lesson Book	Games Book	Theory Workbook	Solo Book
Summer Evenings	*ledger lines*	40		29	
My Own Song	*improvising on G A B C D*	42		31	
Pop!		43	38	32	28
Go To Sleep	*pp*	44		34	
Jig	*1st & 2nd endings*	45	39	35	30
Go For The Gold		46	40	37	
Audio Track List		48			

* Students can check pieces as they play them.

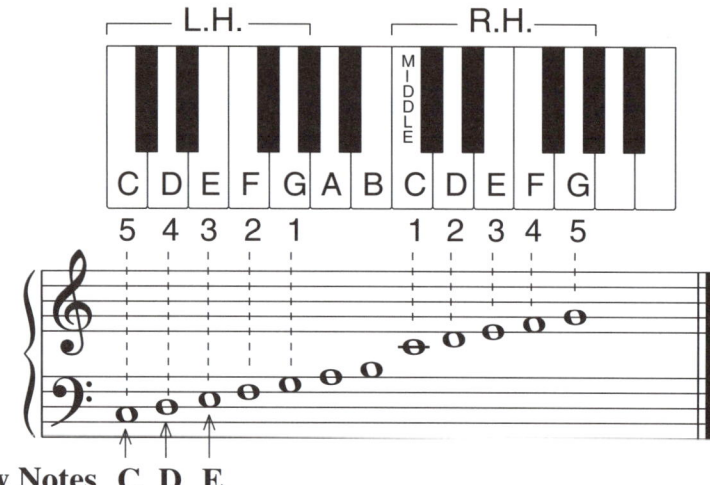

New Notes C D E

Remember,

Whenever you see
this magnifying glass,
fill in the name of the
note.

Reflection

Barbara Kreader

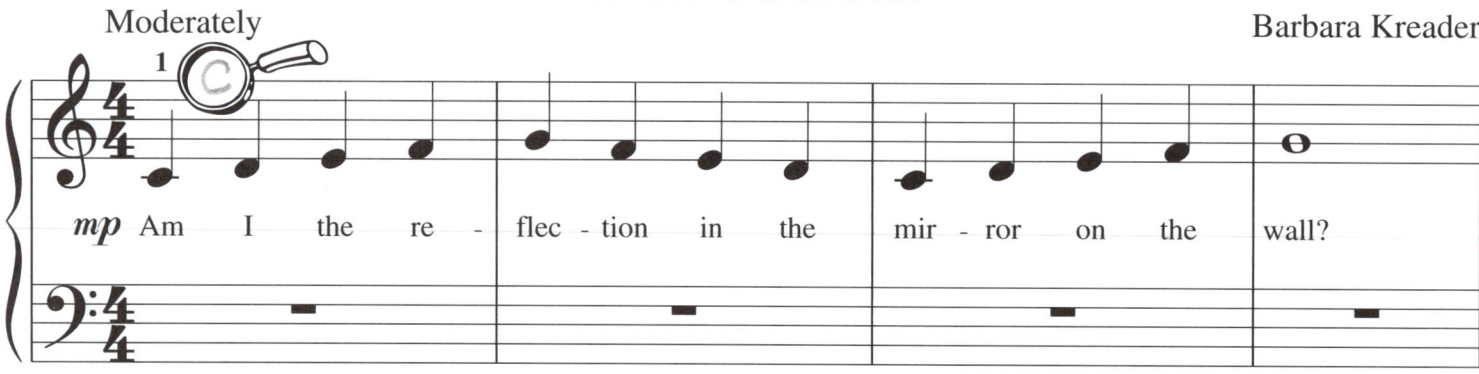

Moderately

mp Am I the re - flec - tion in the mir - ror on the wall?

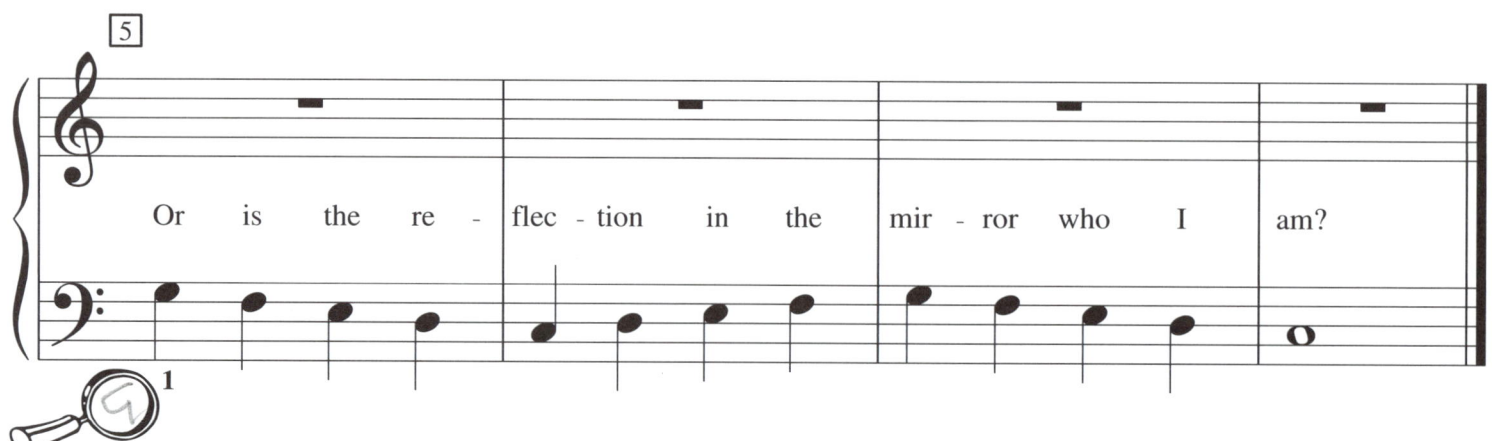

Or is the re - flec - tion in the mir - ror who I am?

Accompaniment (Student plays one octave higher than written.)

Moderately ($\quarternote$=120)

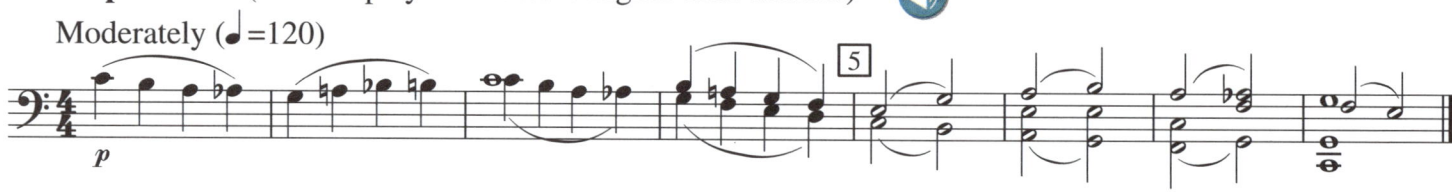

My Own Song
On C D E F G

Place both hands on C D E F G. Listen and feel the pulse as your teacher plays the accompaniment below.

With your right hand, play C D E F G and then play G F E D C. Experiment by mixing the letters any way you want and make up your own song!

With your left hand, play C D E F G and then play G F E D C. Again, mix the letters any way you want and make up another song!

Have fun!

Accompaniment

Moderately (♩=120)

Repeat as necessary   *Last time*

Ode To Joy

Ludwig van Beethoven
(1770–1827)
Adapted by Fred Kern

With majesty

Accompaniment (Student plays one octave higher than written.)

With majesty (♩=105)

6

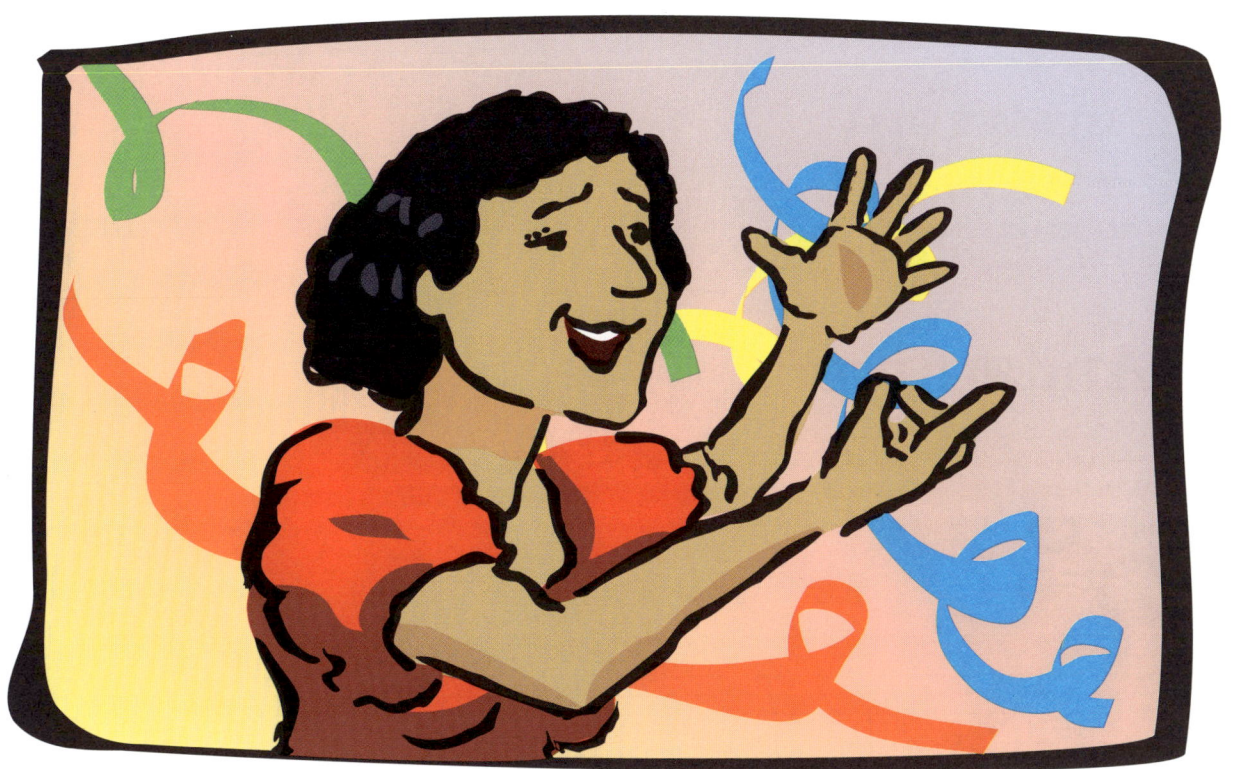

Carmen's Tune

Georges Bizet
(1838–1875)
Adapted by Fred Kern

Lively

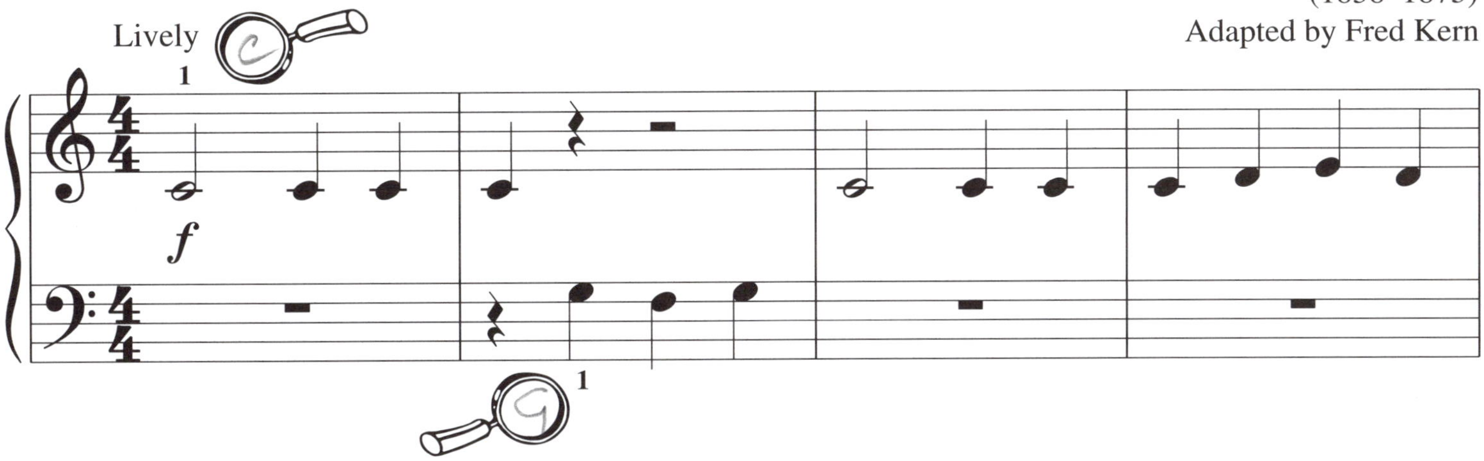

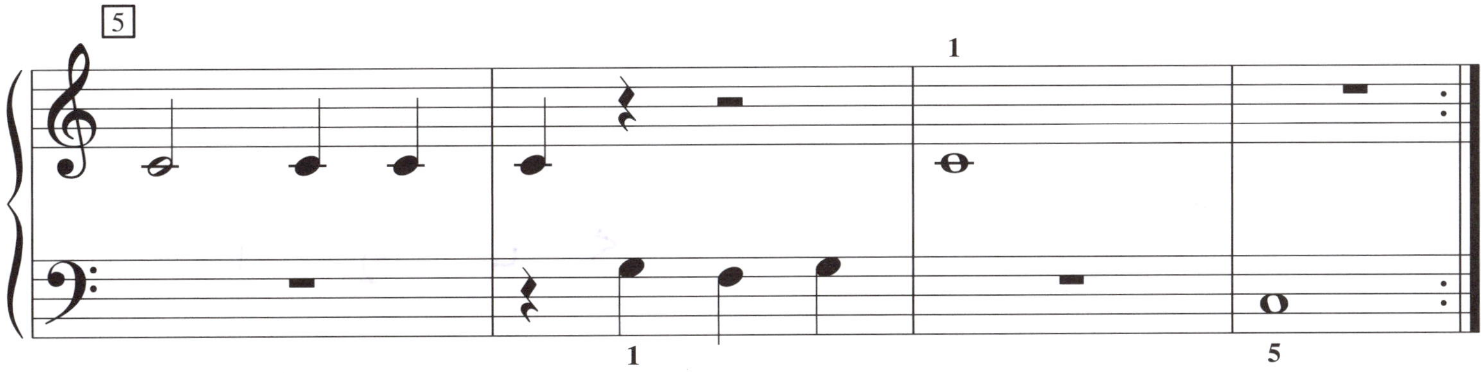

Accompaniment (Student plays one octave higher than written.)

Lively (♩=230)

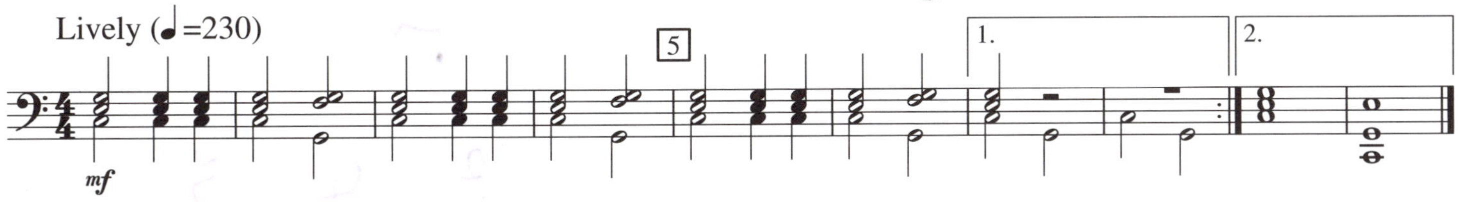

Remember,

$\frac{3}{4}$ **TIME SIGNATURE**

3 = three beats fill every bar
4 = crotchet note gets one beat

LEGATO

When notes sound smooth and connected, they are **Legato**.

A curved line over or under several notes (slur) means **Legato**.

To play **Legato**, pass the sound smoothly from one finger to the next.

Andantino

*Andantino

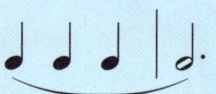

Louis Köhler
(1820–1886)
Adapted by Fred Kern

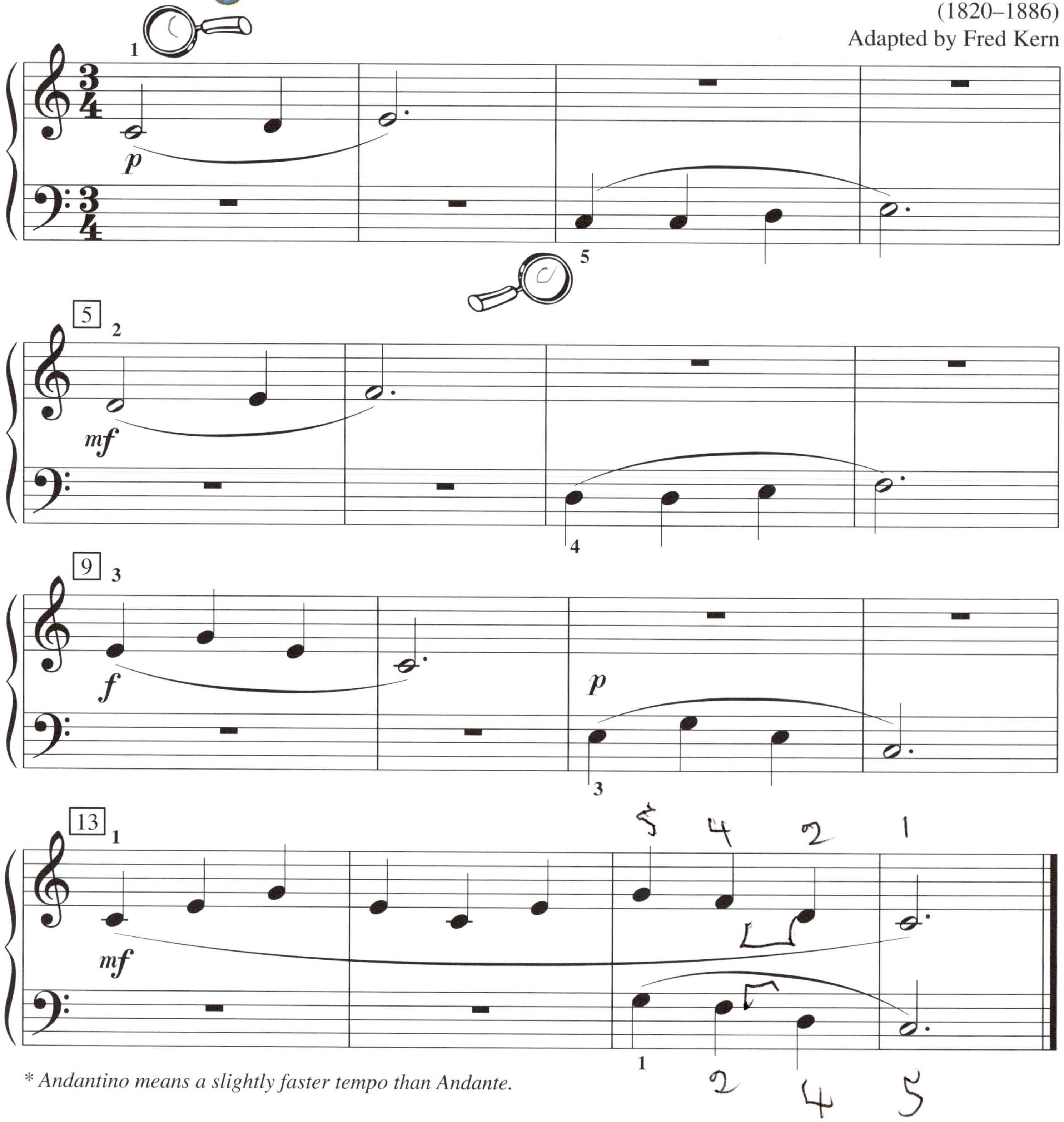

* *Andantino means a slightly faster tempo than Andante.*

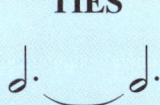
Big Ben

Steady (♩=120)

Traditional

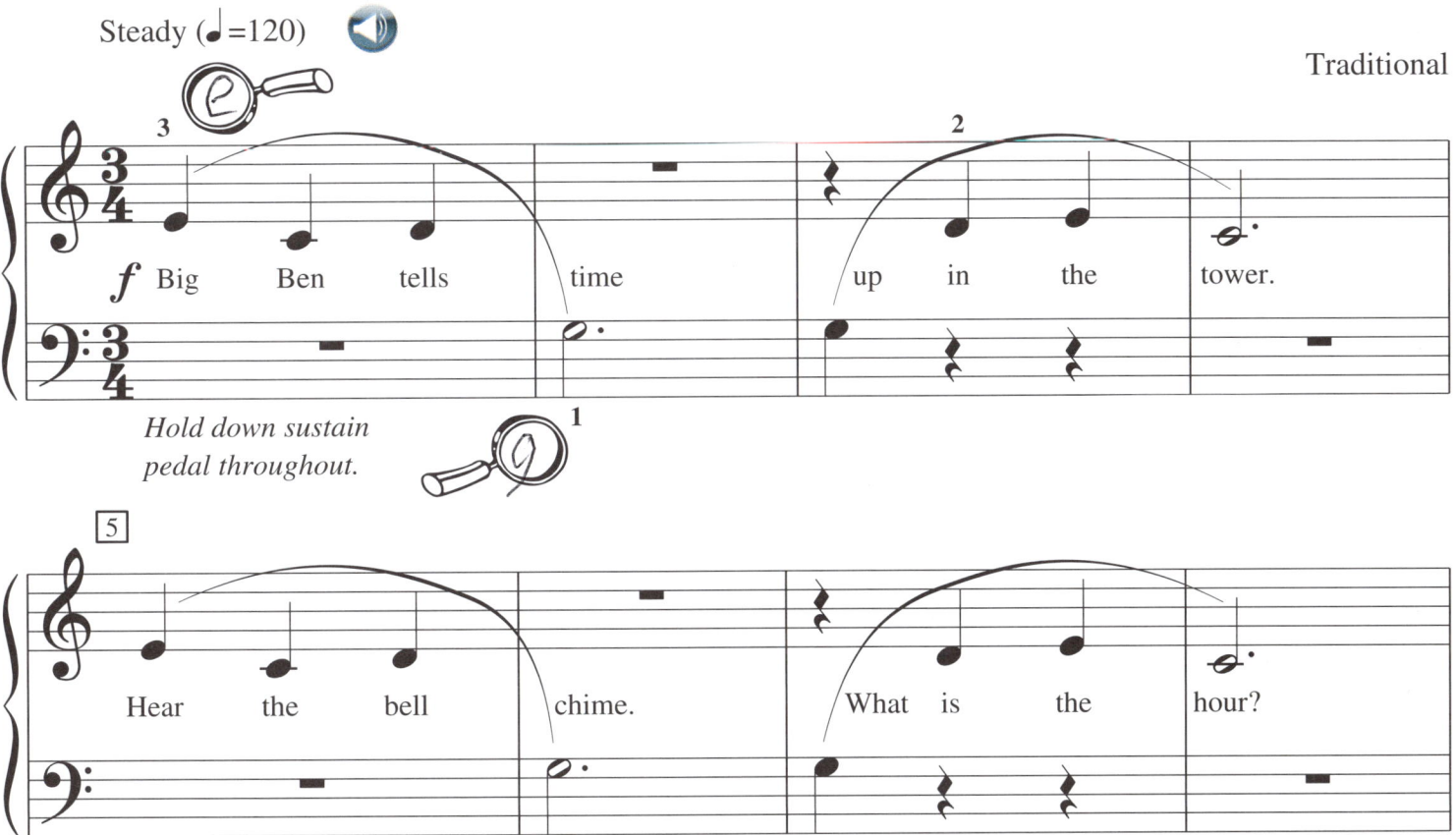

Big   Ben   tells   time   up   in   the   tower.

Hold down sustain pedal throughout.

Hear   the   bell   chime.   What   is   the   hour?

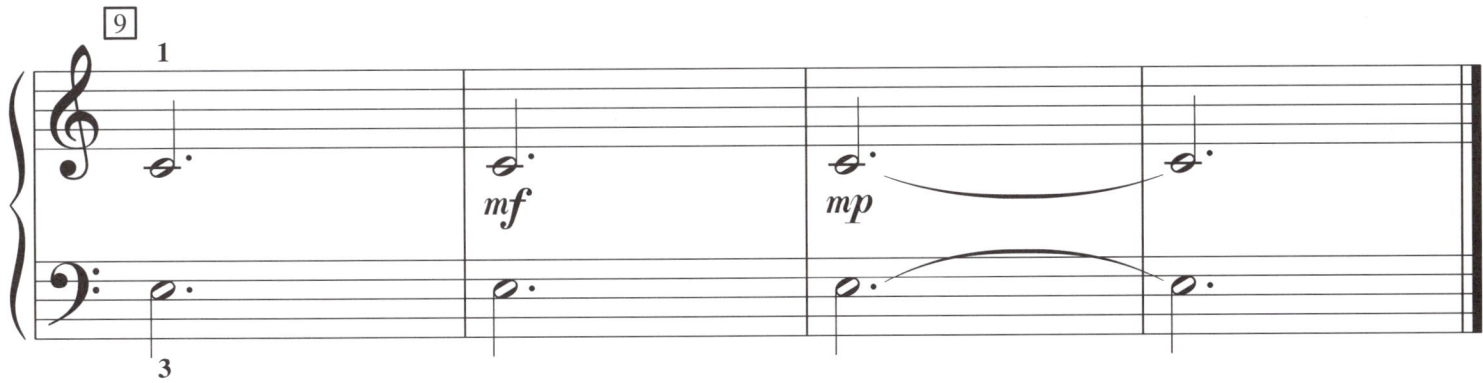

INTERVAL

An **Interval** is the distance from one key to another key.

Interval of a 2nd	Interval of a 3rd

Melodic Intervals – Notes played one after the other make a melody.
Harmonic Intervals – Notes played together make harmony.

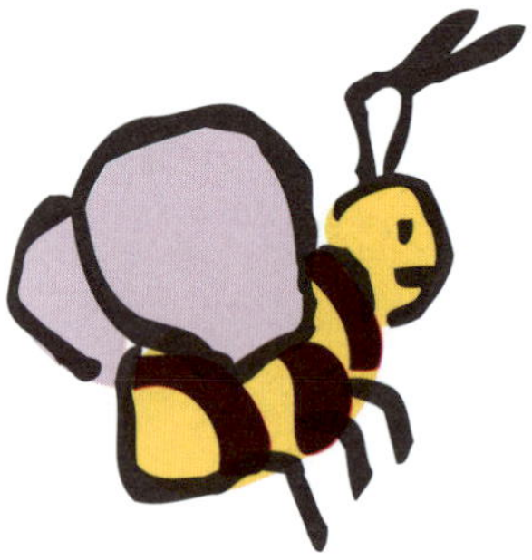

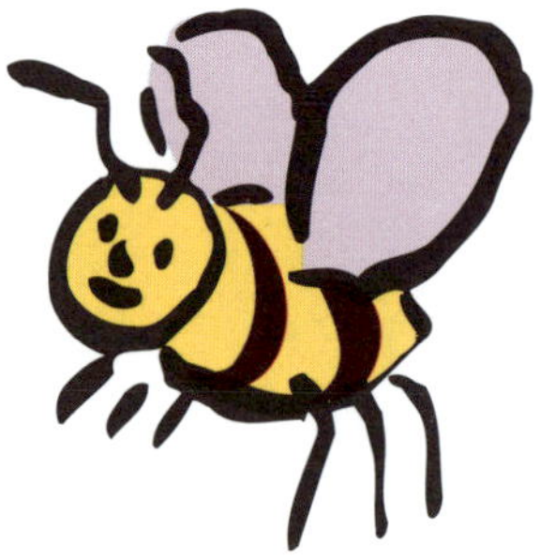

With your left hand play:

Melodic 2nds
Harmonic 2nds
Melodic 3rds
Harmonic 3rds

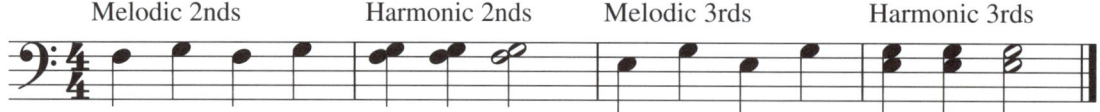

Please, No Bees!

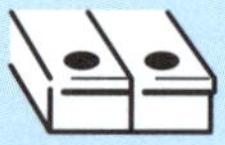

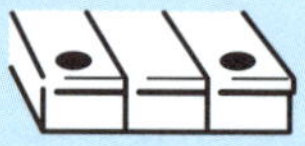

Cranky (♩=155)

Barbara Kreader

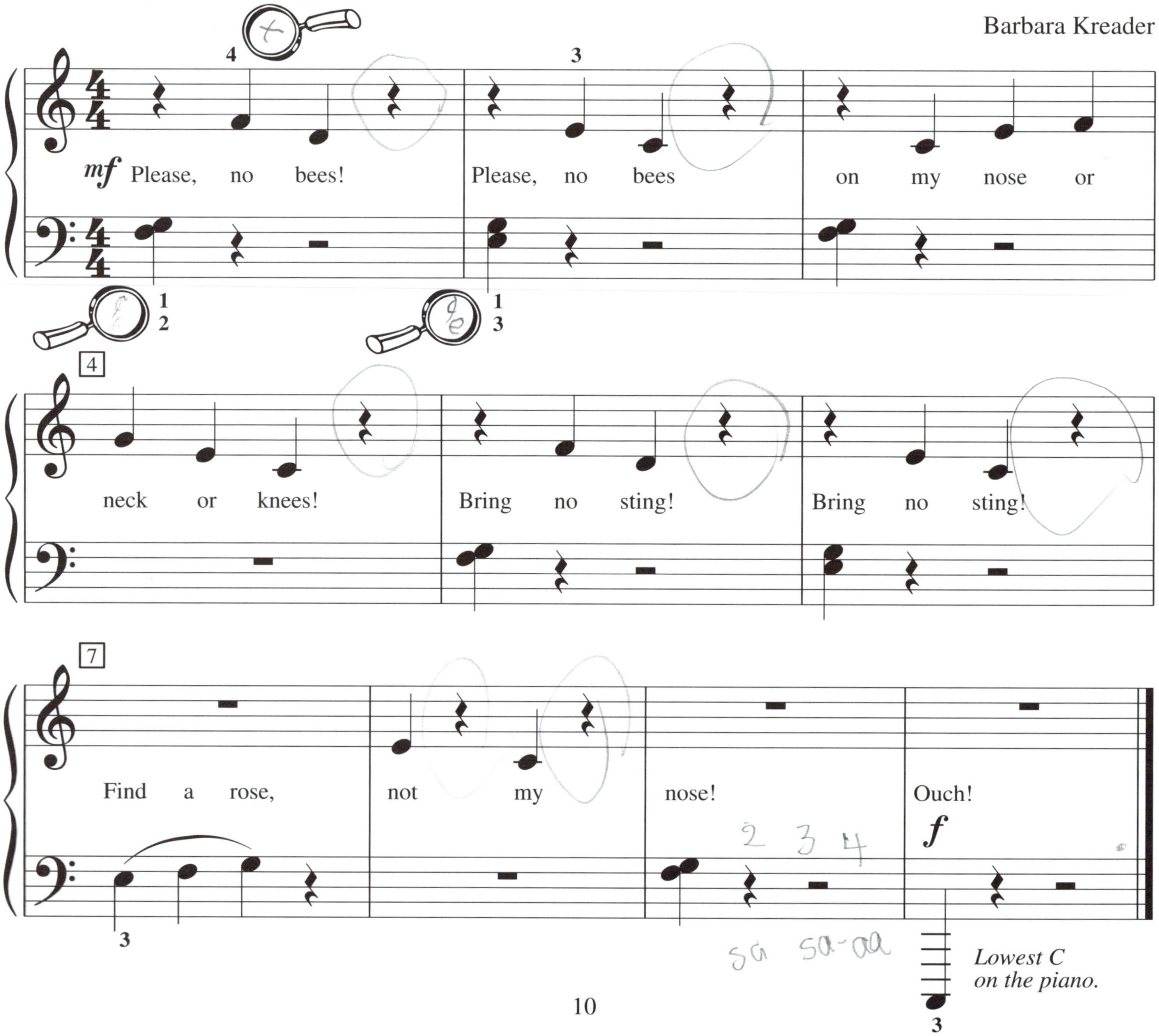

mf Please, no bees! Please, no bees on my nose or
neck or knees! Bring no sting! Bring no sting!
Find a rose, not my nose! Ouch!
f
Lowest C
on the piano.

Clapping Song

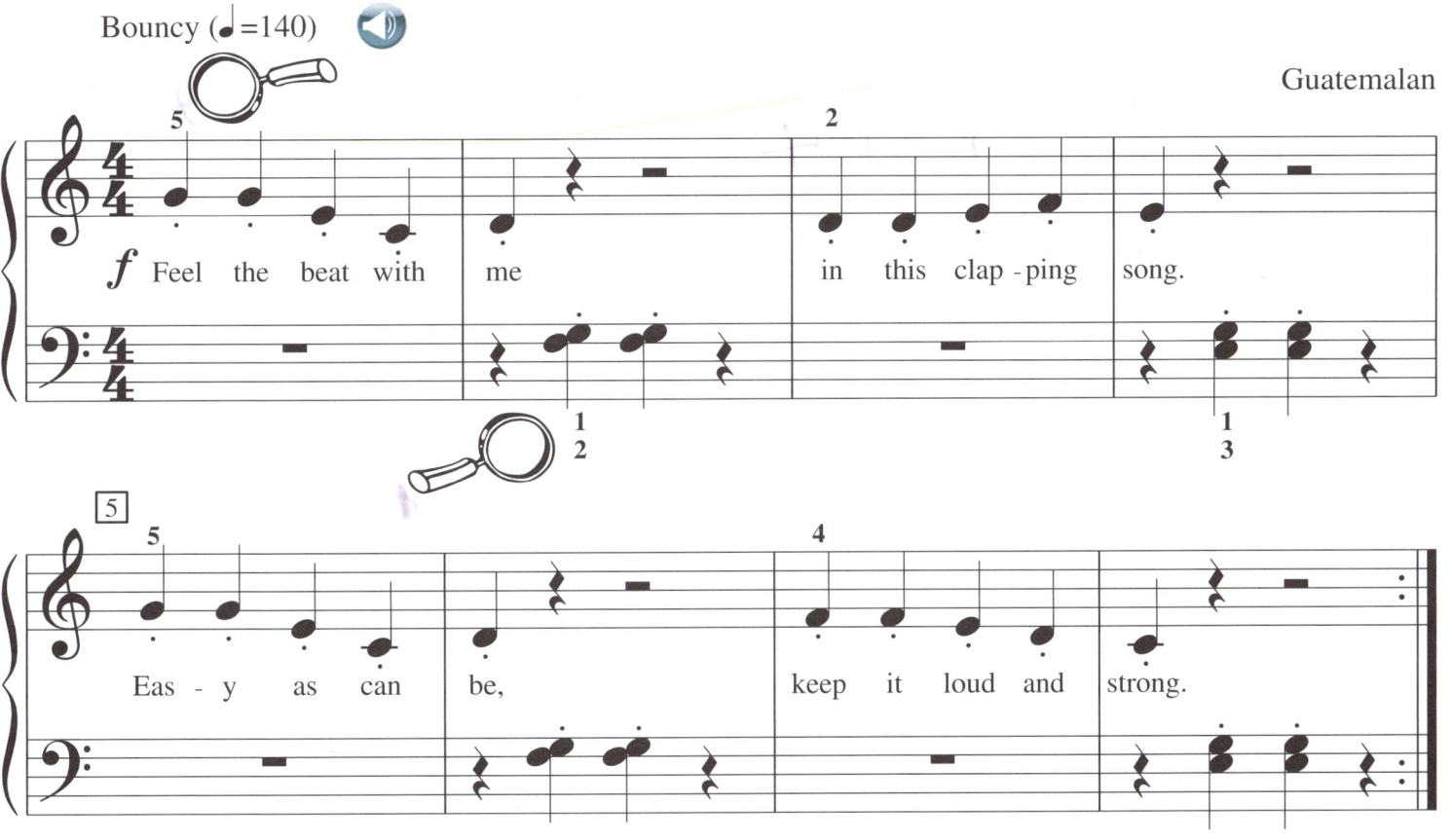

Bouncy (♩=140)

Guatemalan

f Feel the beat with me   in this clap-ping song.

Eas-y   as can   be,   keep it loud and strong.

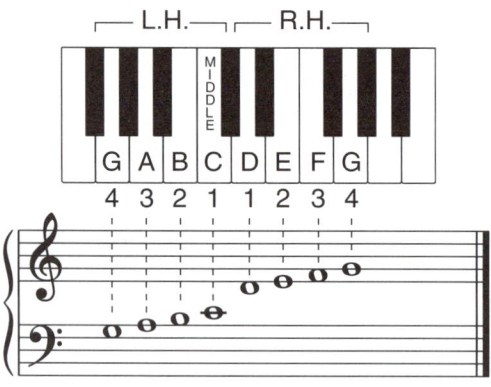

INTERVAL of a 4th

On the piano, a 4th
- skips two keys
- skips two fingers
- skips two letters

On the staff, a 4th
- skips two notes from either a line to a space or a space to a line.

Hoedown

Janet Medley

Toe tappin'

f At the hoe - down, do - si - do, all our friends will meet.

Swing your part - ner, don't be slow. Clap your hands and stomp your feet!

Accompaniment (Student plays one octave higher than written.)

Toe tappin' (♩=150)

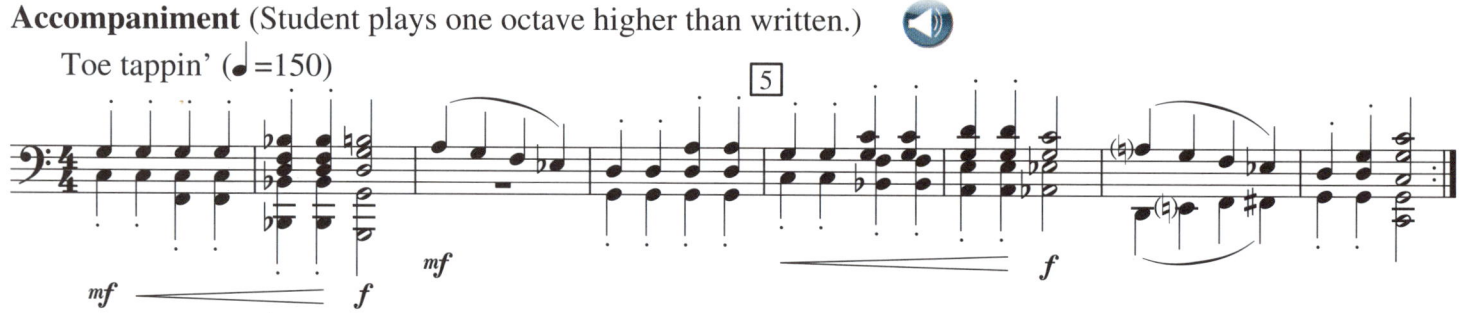

mf *f* *mf* *f*

12

Sunlight Through The Trees

Flowing (♩=120)

Phillip Keveren

Play one octave higher than written and hold down sustain pedal throughout.

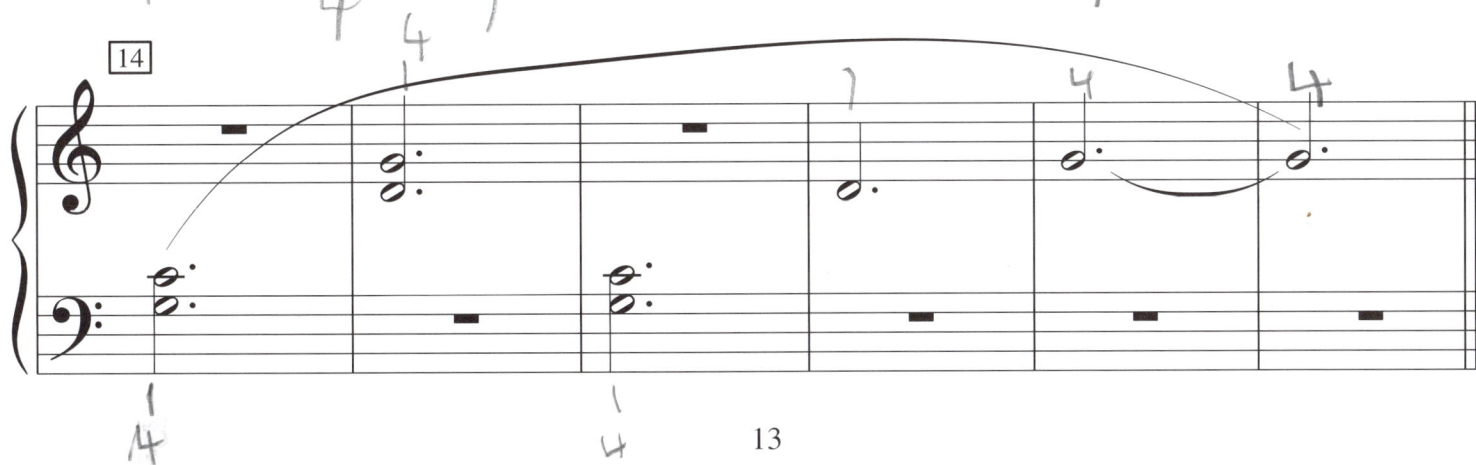

13

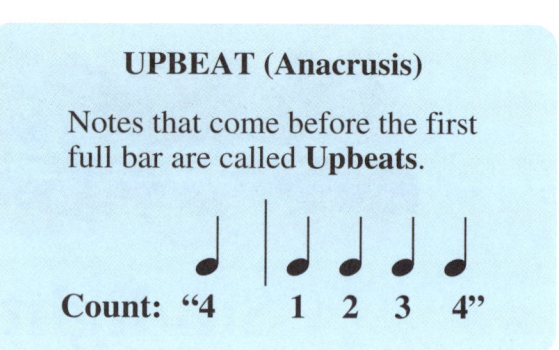

Bingo

Bouncy

Traditional

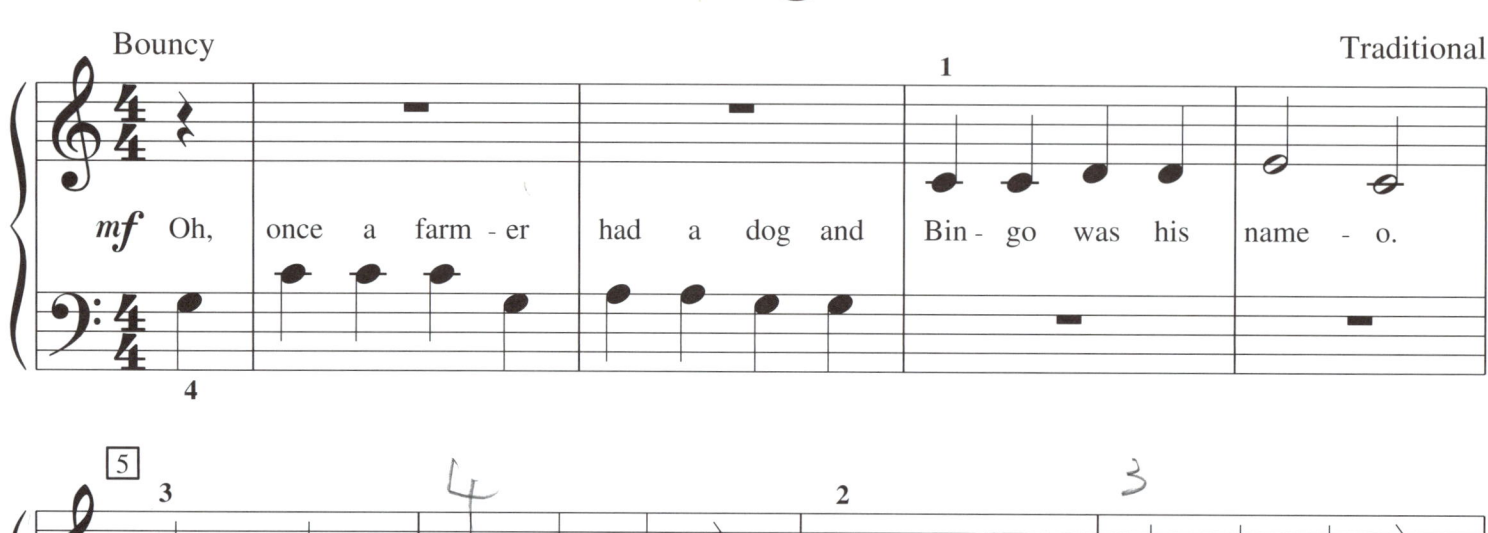

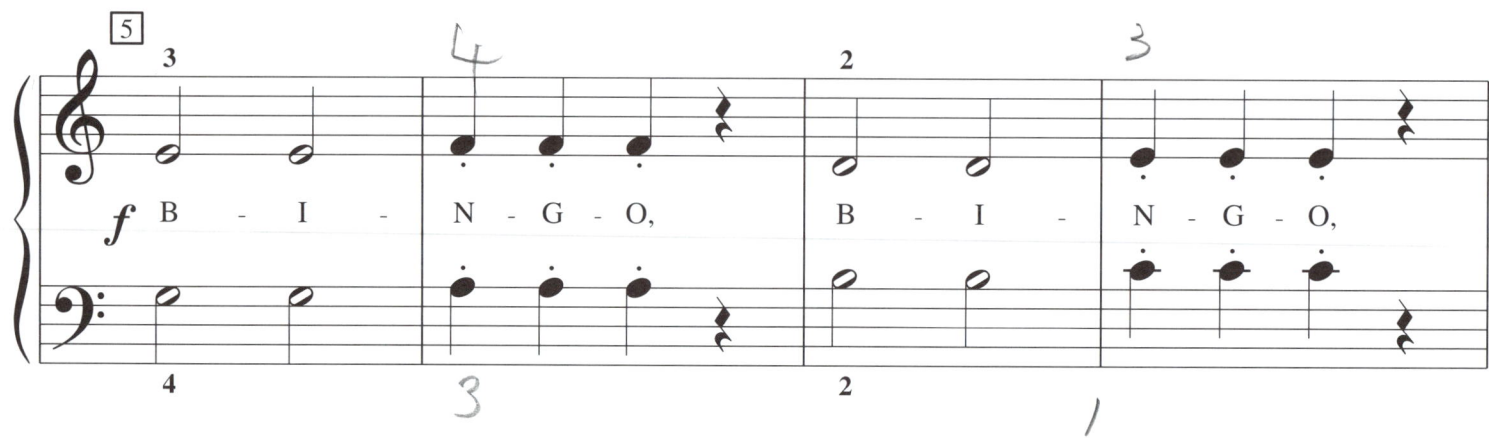

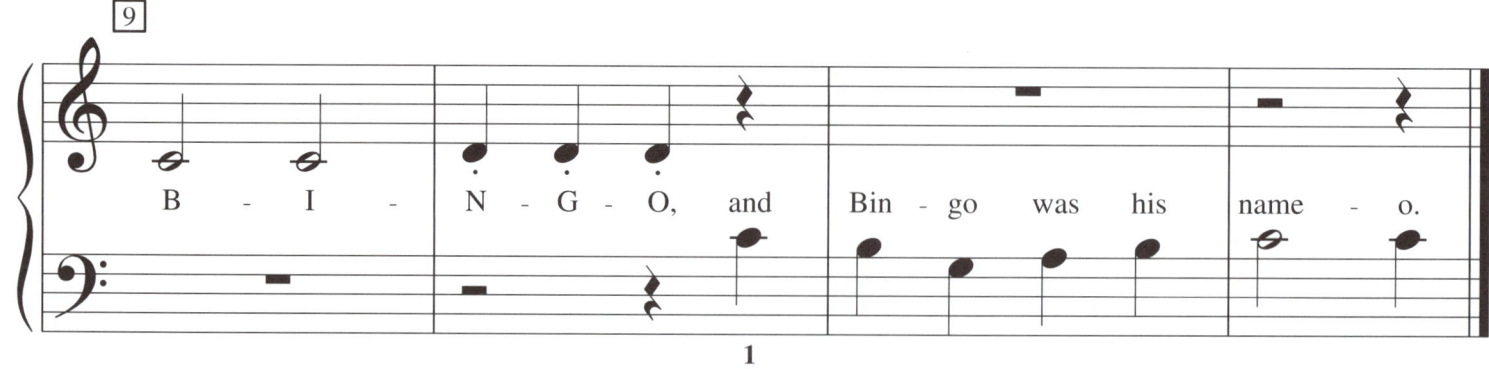

Accompaniment (Student plays one octave higher than written.)

Bouncy (♩=140)

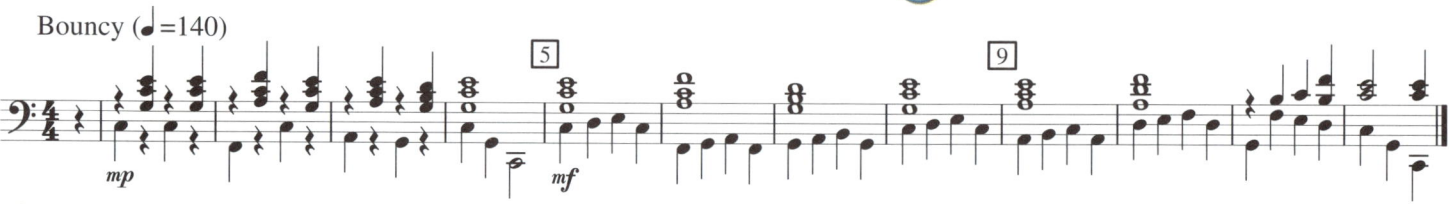

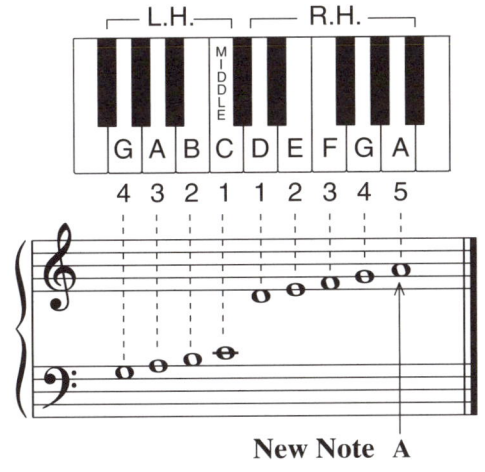

New Note A

Travelling Along
The Prairie

Italo Taranta

Moving along

mf

Accompaniment (Student plays one octave higher than written.)

Moving along (♩=145)

mp

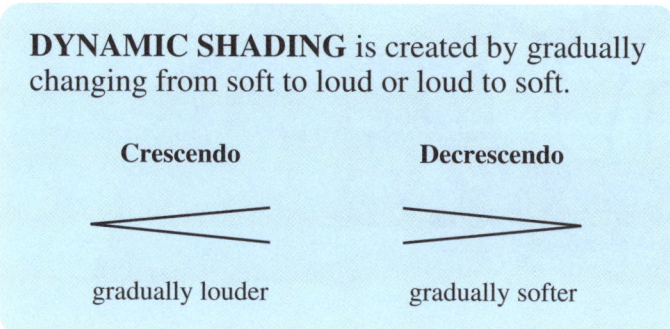

DYNAMIC SHADING is created by gradually changing from soft to loud or loud to soft.

Crescendo

gradually louder

Decrescendo

gradually softer

No One To Walk With

Slowly

Italo Taranta

Accompaniment (Student plays one octave higher than written.)

Slowly ($\quad$=100)

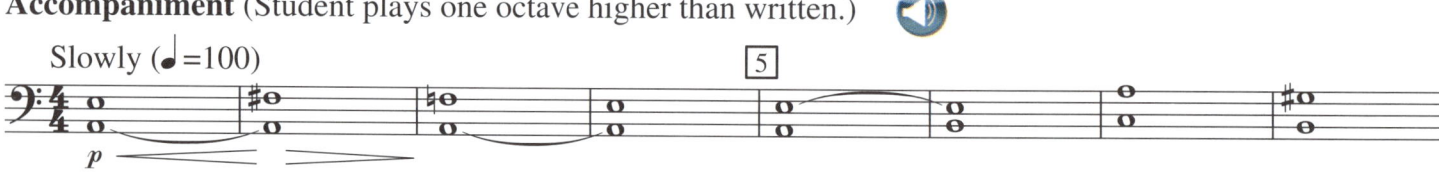

16

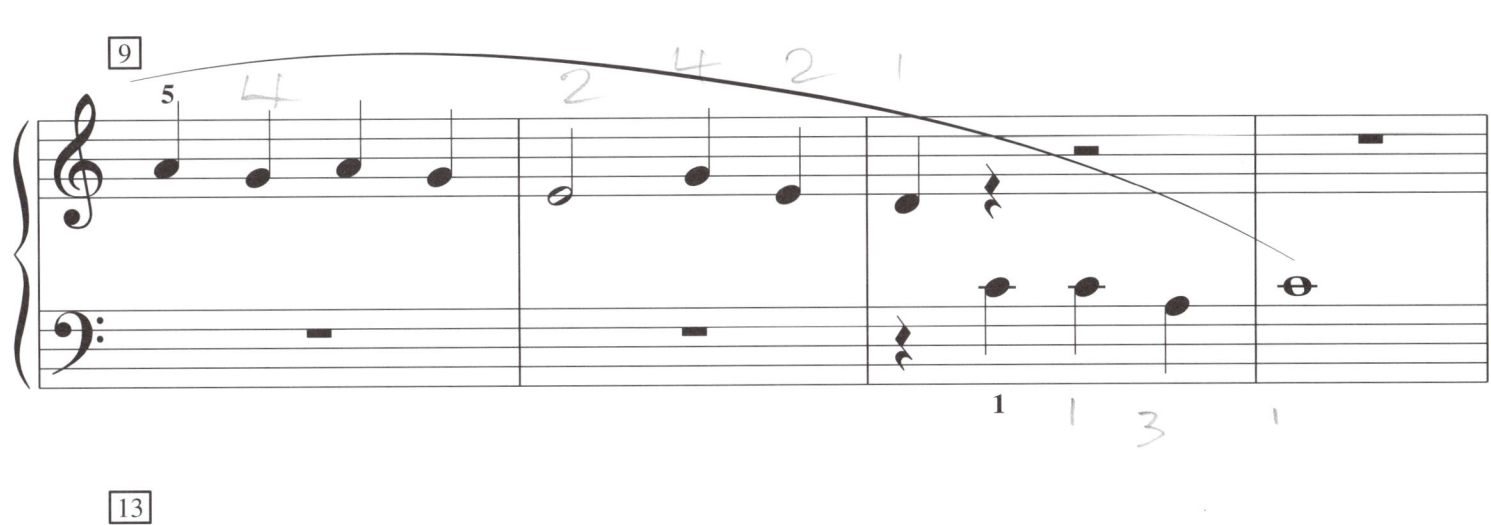

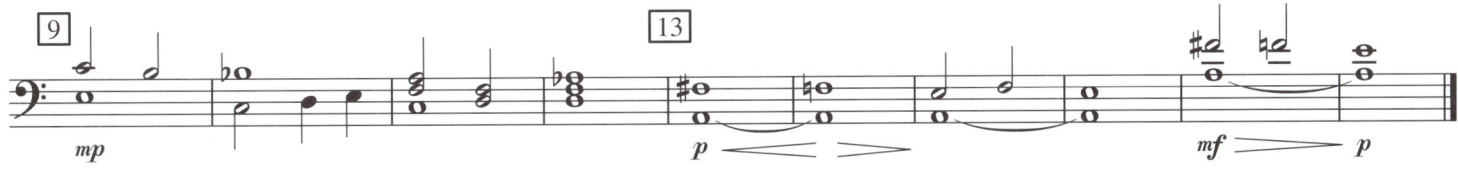

Painted Rocking Horse

Dreamlike

Phillip Keveren

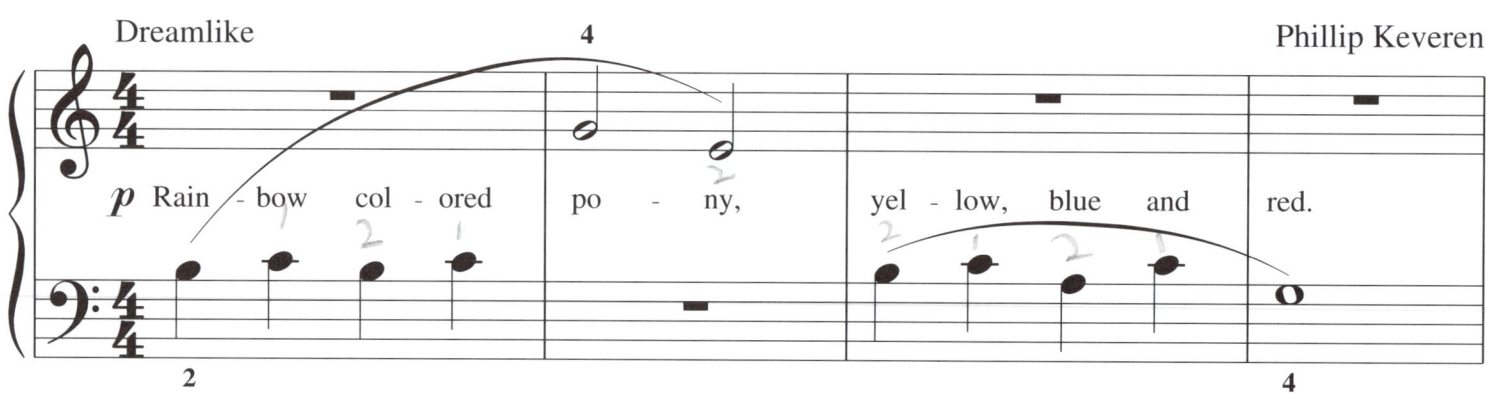

p Rain - bow col - ored po - ny, yel - low, blue and red.

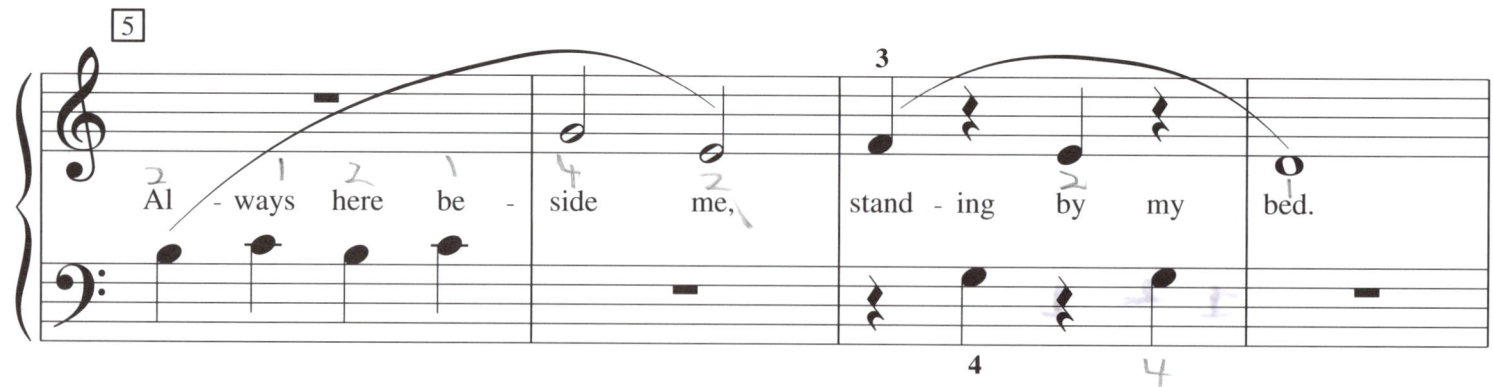

Al - ways here be - side me, stand - ing by my bed.

Accompaniment (Student plays two octaves higher than written.)

Dreamlike (♩=95)

With pedal

18

When the sky is cloud - y, you and I can play,

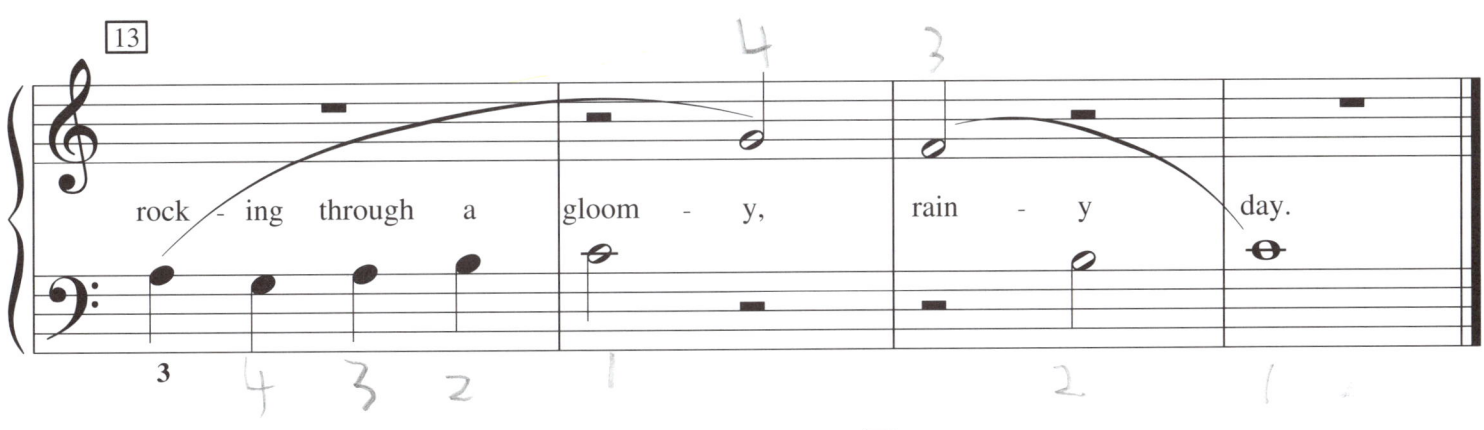

rock - ing through a gloom - y, rain - y day.

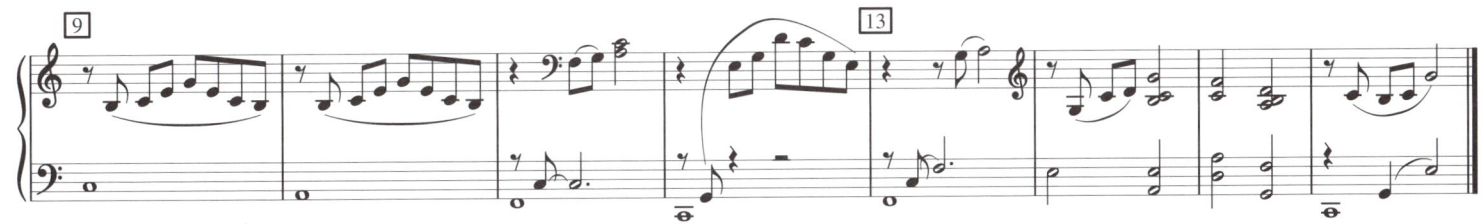

Tick Tock The Jazz Clock

With a steady beat like the tick of a clock

Bill Boyd

Accompaniment

With a steady beat (♩=120) (♫ = ♩♪)

mp

20

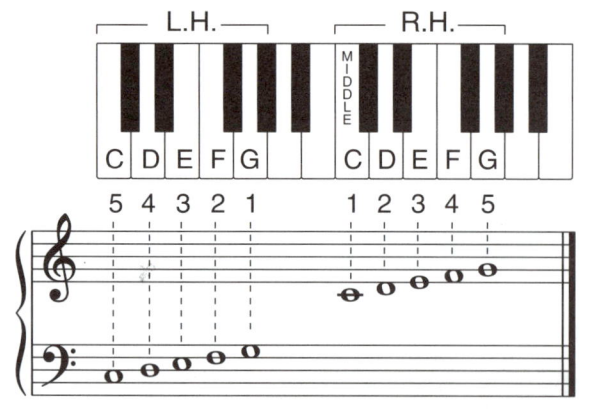

On the piano, a 5th
- skips three keys
- skips three fingers
- skips three letters

On the staff, a 5th
- skips three notes from either a line to a line or a space to a space.

Watercolors

Delicately (♩=105)

Phillip Keveren

Play one octave higher than written and hold down sustain pedal throughout.

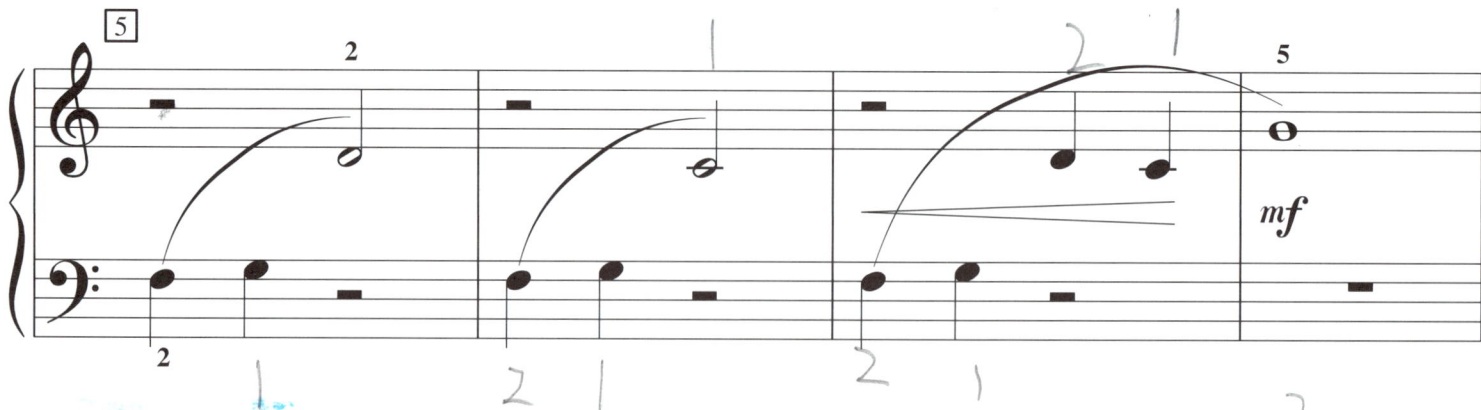

Let it ring!

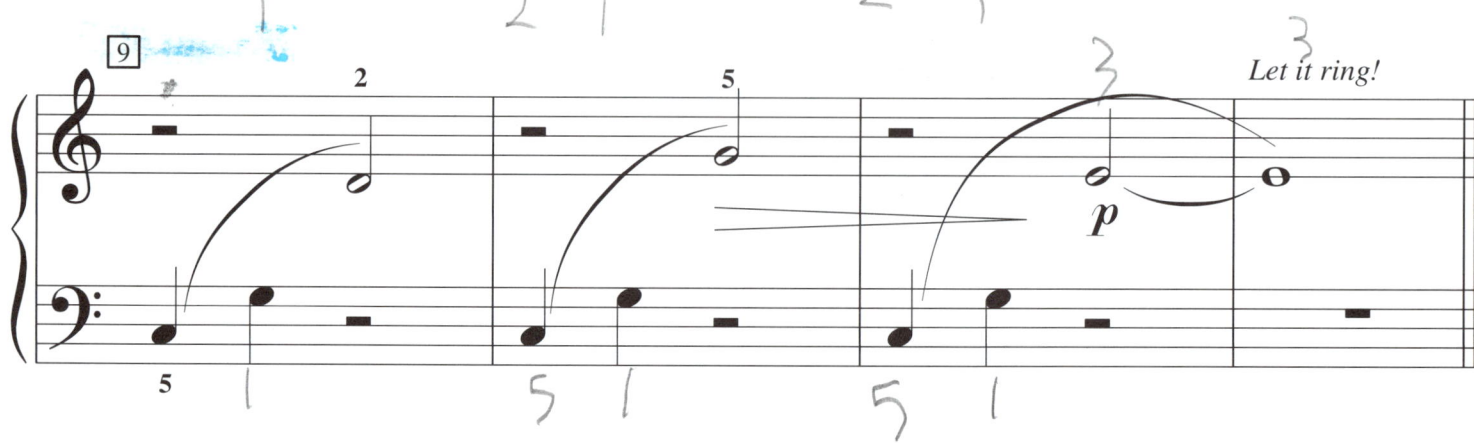

22

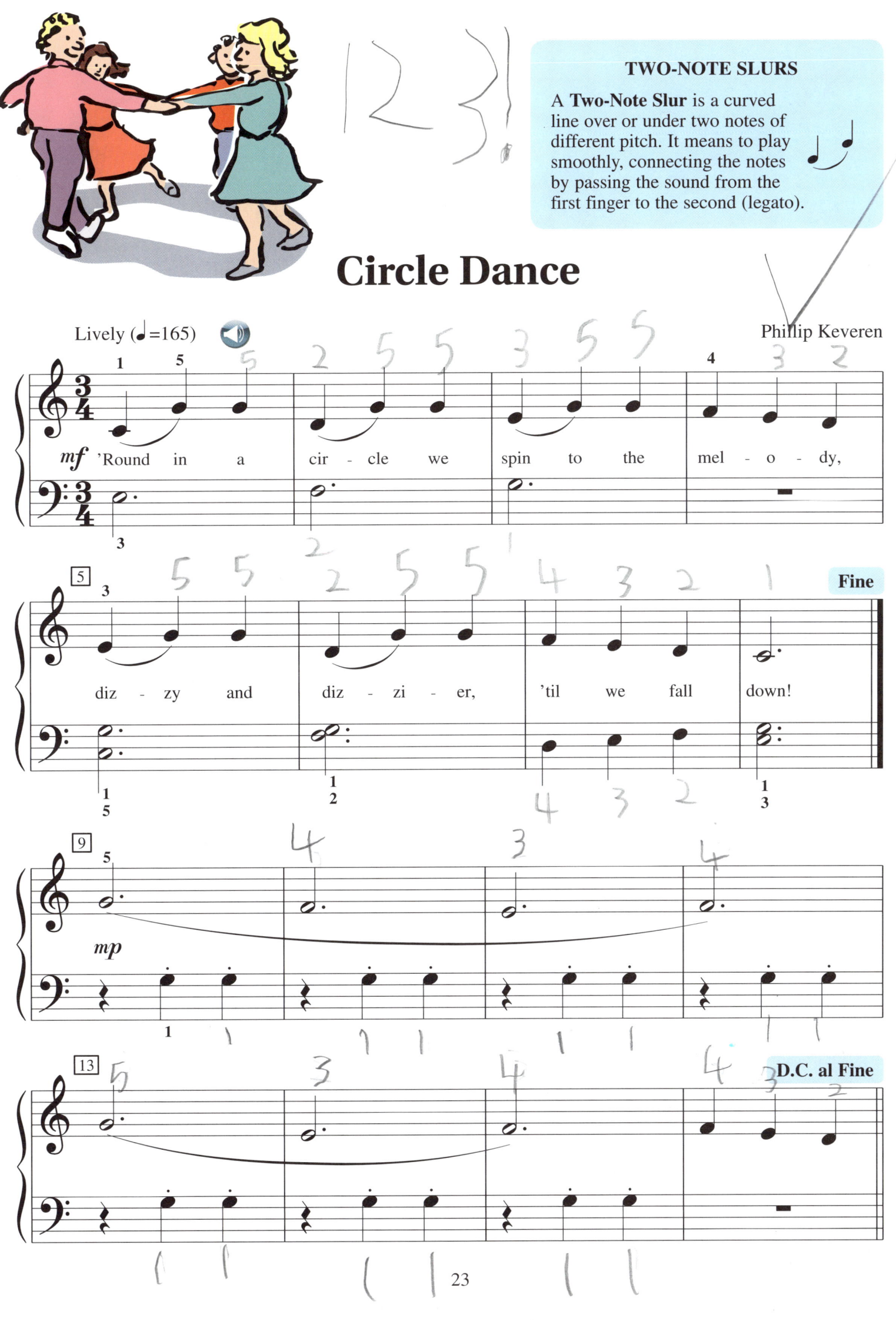

TWO-NOTE SLURS

A **Two-Note Slur** is a curved line over or under two notes of different pitch. It means to play smoothly, connecting the notes by passing the sound from the first finger to the second (legato).

Circle Dance

Lively (♩=165)

Phillip Keveren

'Round in a cir - cle we spin to the mel - o - dy,

diz - zy and diz - zi - er, 'til we fall down!

Basketball Bounce

Tempo de dribble (With energy!) (♩=190)

Phillip Keveren

Allegro

Anton Diabelli
(1781–1858)
Adapted by Fred Kern

25

8va ---┘

When the sign *8va---┘* appears under a note or group of notes, play the note or notes one octave lower than written.

FORTISSIMO

_ff_

means very loud.

Great News!

Great ☺ 10 - 8 - 17

With excitement! (♩=170)

Bruce Berr

f

ff

26

8va - ┘

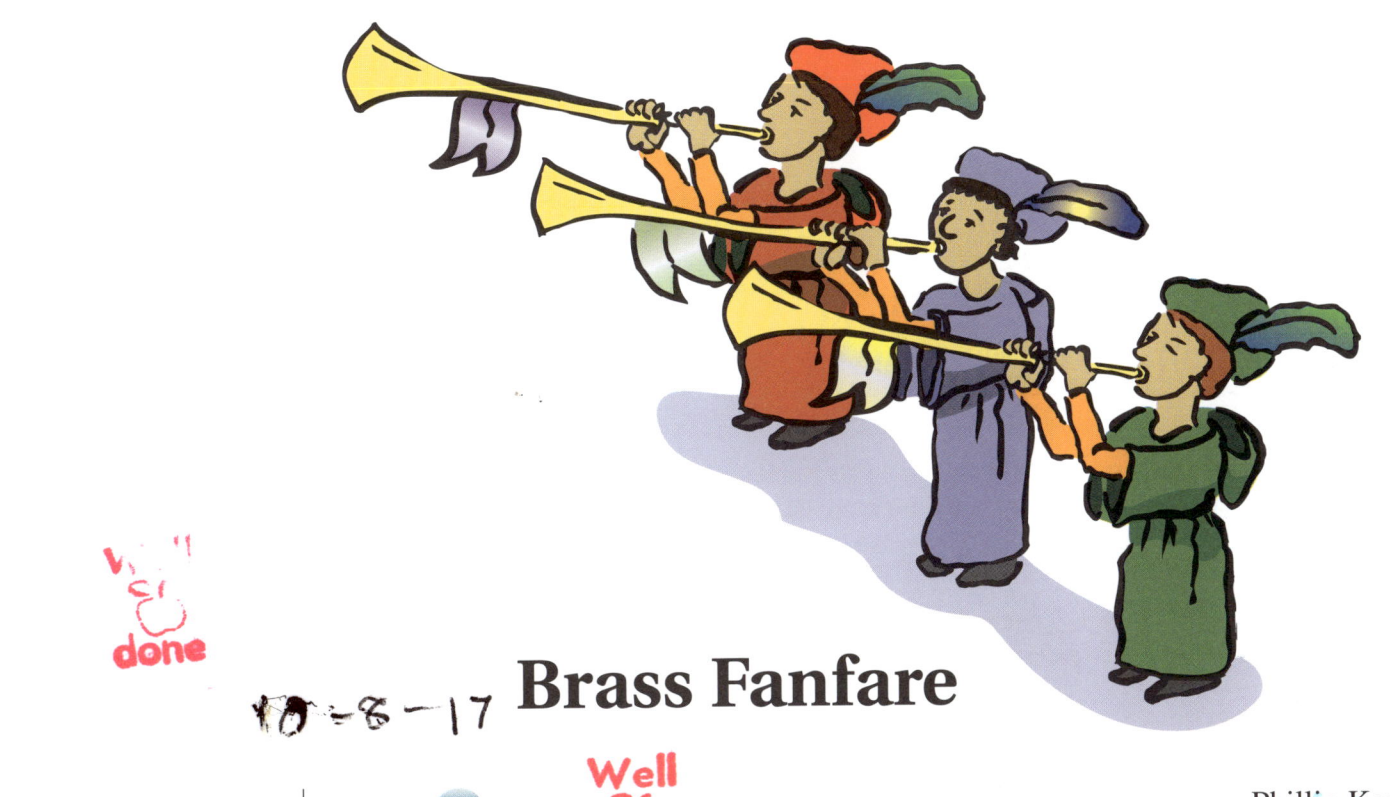

Well done

10-8-17

Brass Fanfare

Triumphantly (♩=110)

Phillip Keveren

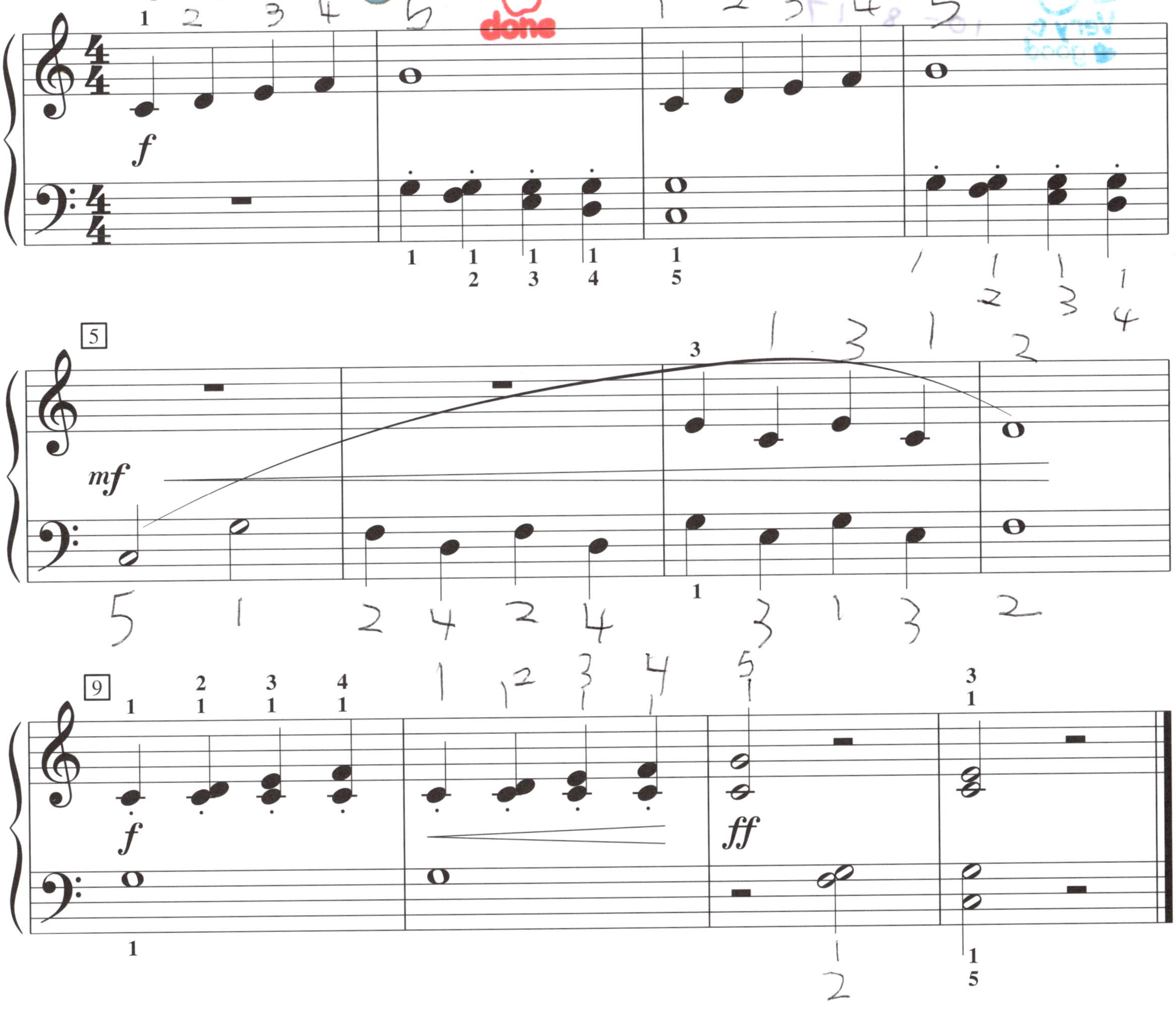

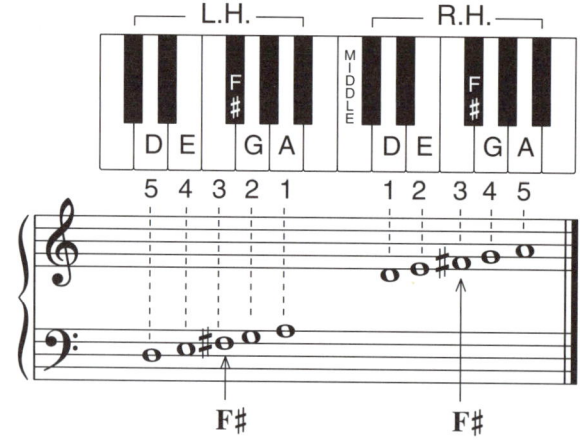

UNIT 4

Little River Flowing

Folk Tune

Accompaniment (Student plays one octave higher than written.)

Smoothly (♩=145)

With pedal

28

Quiet Thoughts

H. Berens
(1826–1880)
Op. 62
Adapted by Fred Kern

Andante

mp

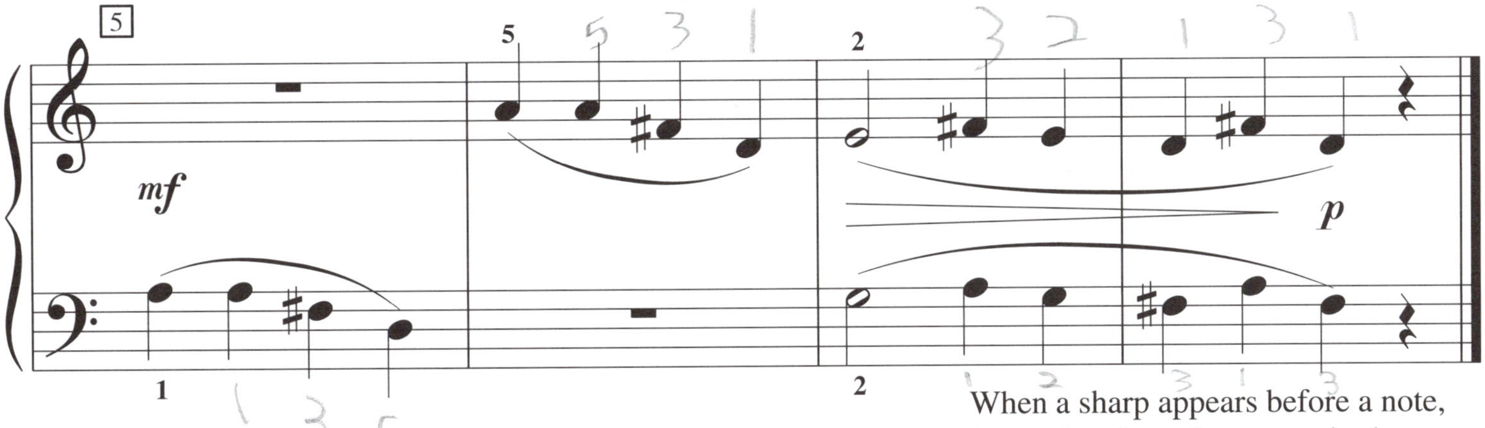

mf

p

When a sharp appears before a note,
it remains sharp for one entire bar.

Accompaniment (Student plays one octave higher than written.)

Andante (♩=120)

p

mp

p

L.H.
R.H.
MIDDLE
C♯
F♯
G A B D E G
5 4 3 2 1 2 3 4
C♯

A B A Form

In "Star Quest," lines one and two are the A section, lines three and four are the B section. After B, you play A one more time.

The form of this piece is A B A.

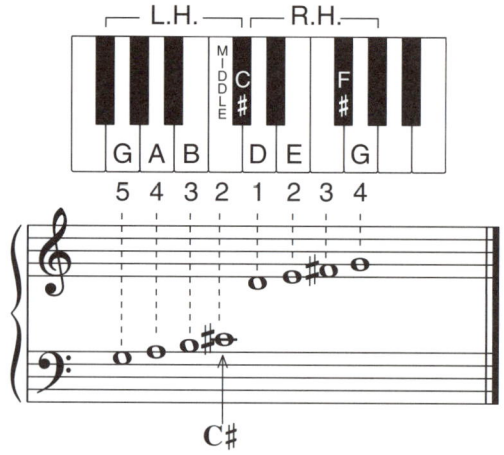

Star Quest

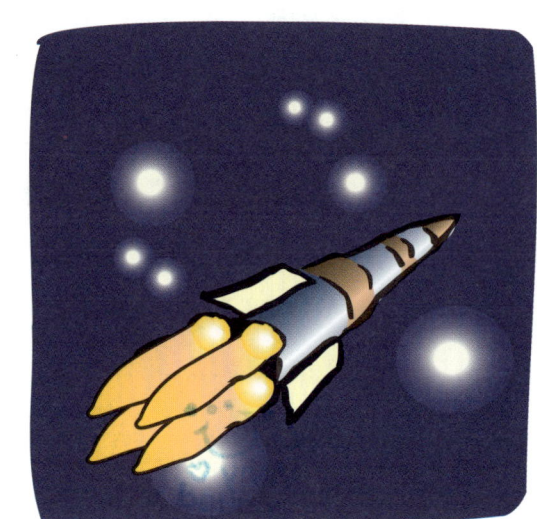

A

Heroic March

Phillip Keveren

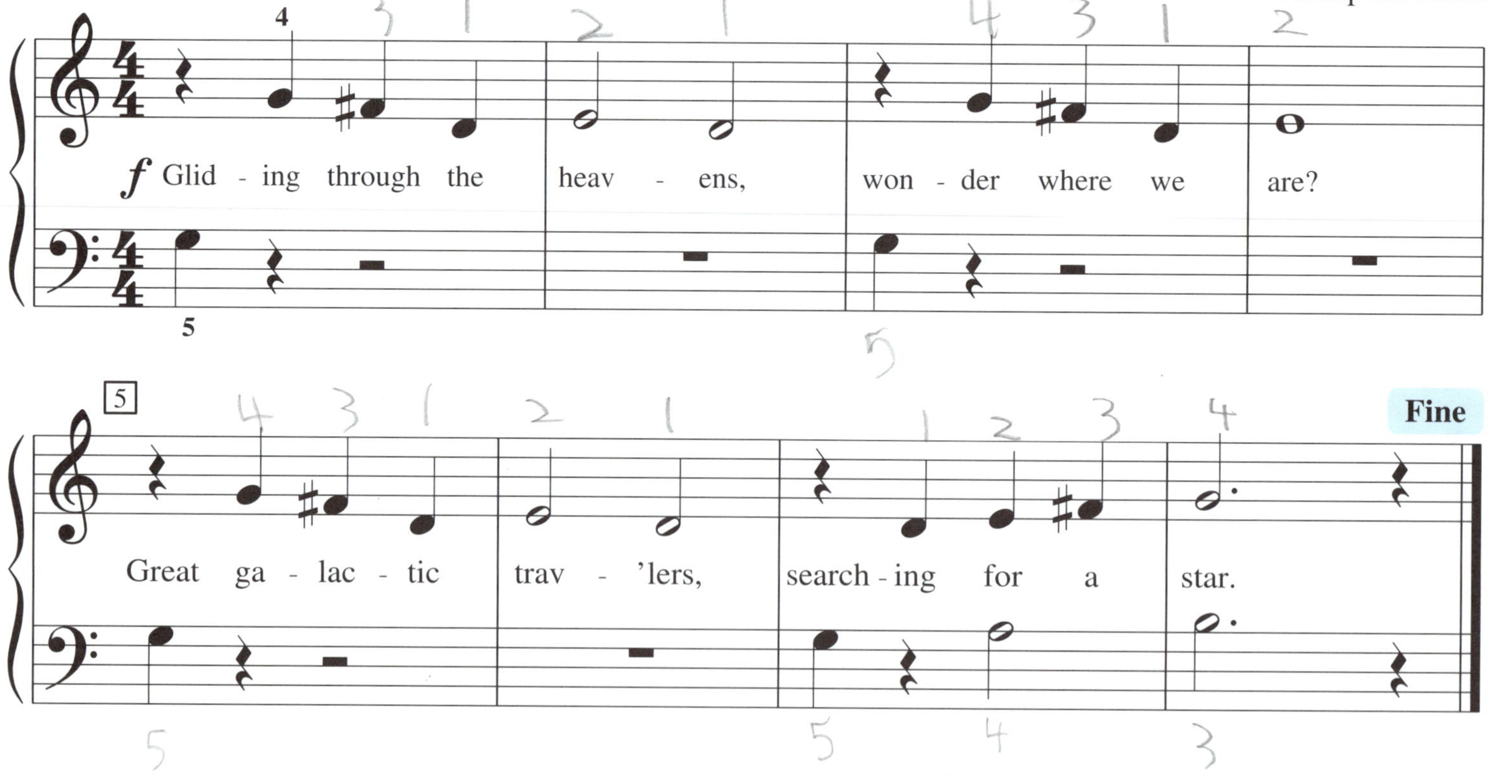

Glid - ing through the heav - ens, won - der where we are?
Great ga - lac - tic trav - 'lers, search - ing for a star.
Fine

Accompaniment (Student plays one octave higher than written.)

Heroic March (♩=120)

mf
Fine

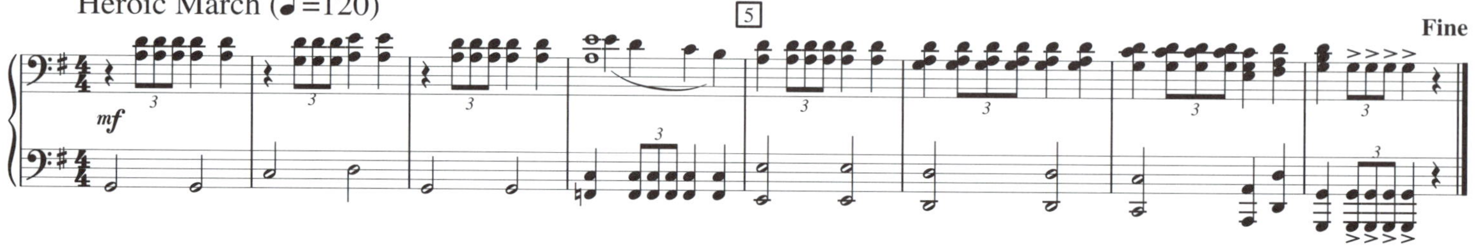

B

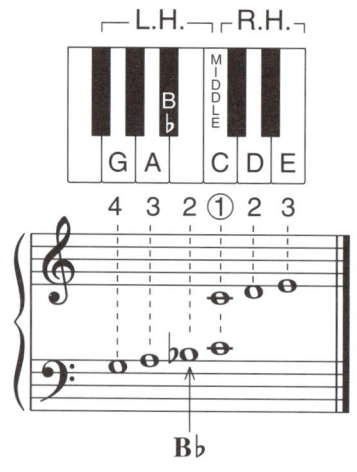

A Little Latin

Moderately fast

Bill Boyd

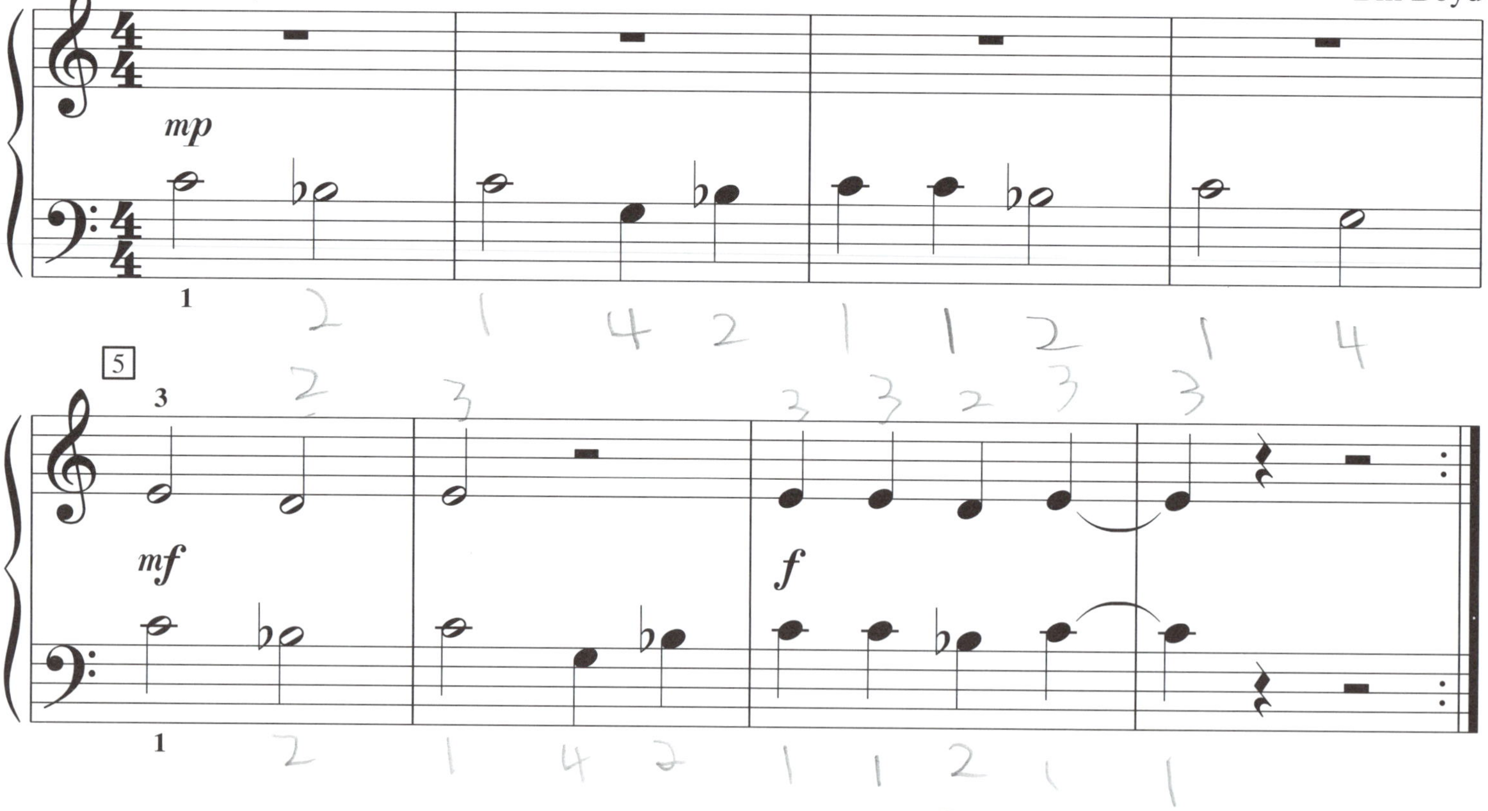

mp

mf

f

Accompaniment (Student plays one octave higher than written.)

Moderately fast (♩=170)

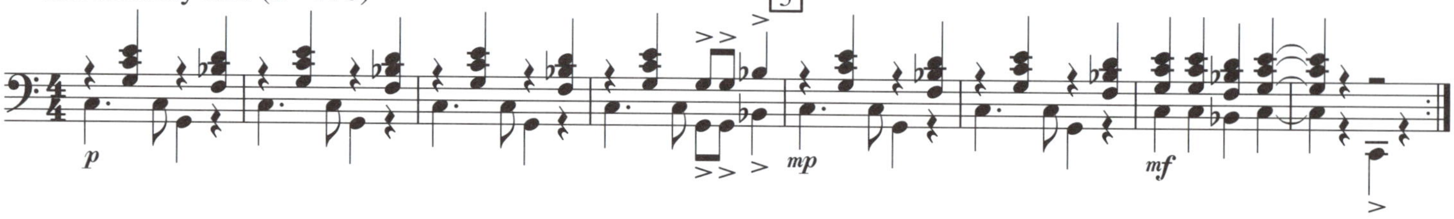

p   *mp*   *mf*

Stompin'

Bill Boyd

ACCENT

>

An **Accent** over or under a note means to play that note louder.

Keep the beat! (♩=190)

D♯ is the same piano key as E♭.

RITARD

Ritard or *rit.* means to slow the tempo gradually.

First Light

Gaelic Melody
Words by Fred Kern

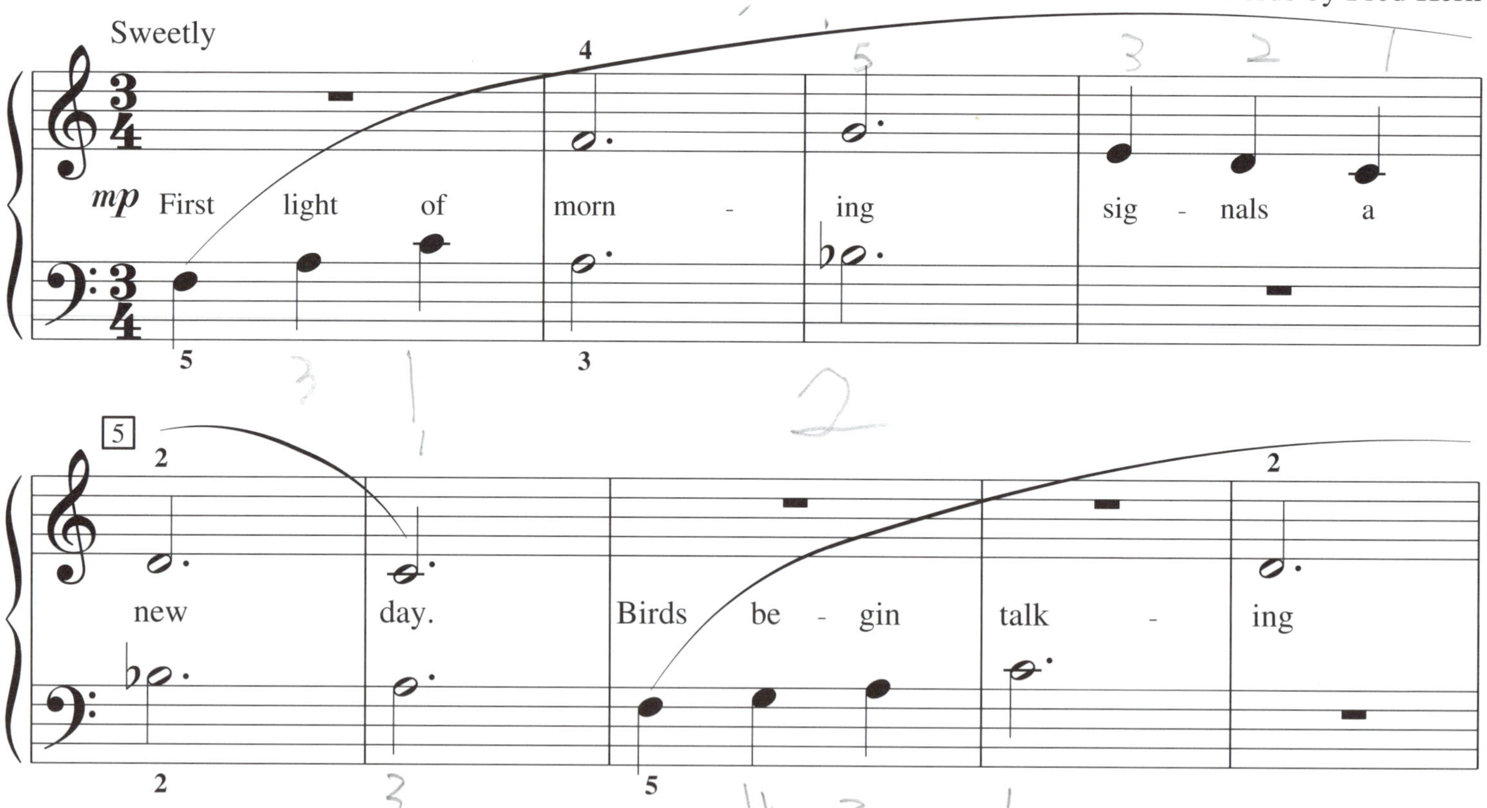

Sweetly

mp First light of morn - ing sig - nals a

new day. Birds be - gin talk - ing

Accompaniment (Student plays one octave higher than written.)

Sweetly (♩=120)

p

Inspector Hound

Phillip Keveren

Sneaky (♩=145)

36

PAUSE (Fermata)

𝄐

A **Pause** means to hold a note longer than its rhythmic value.

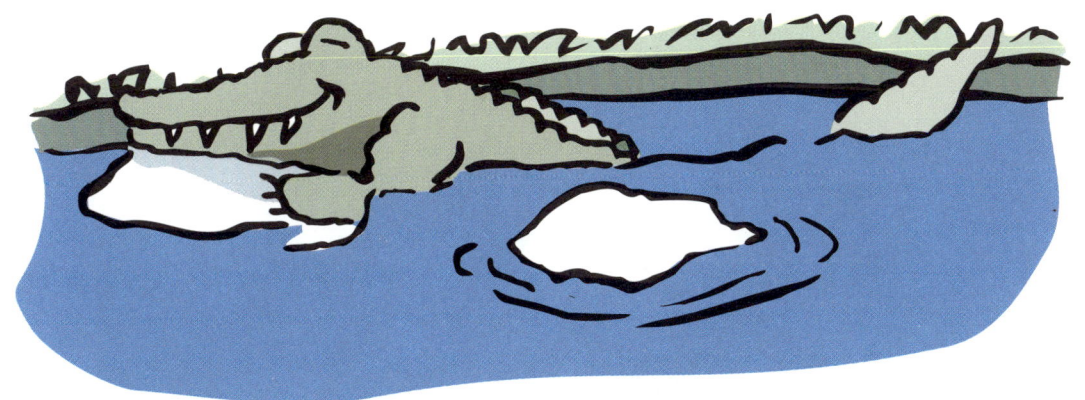

Bayou Blues

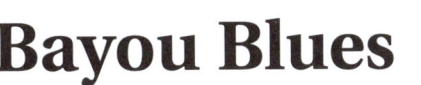

Phillip Keveren

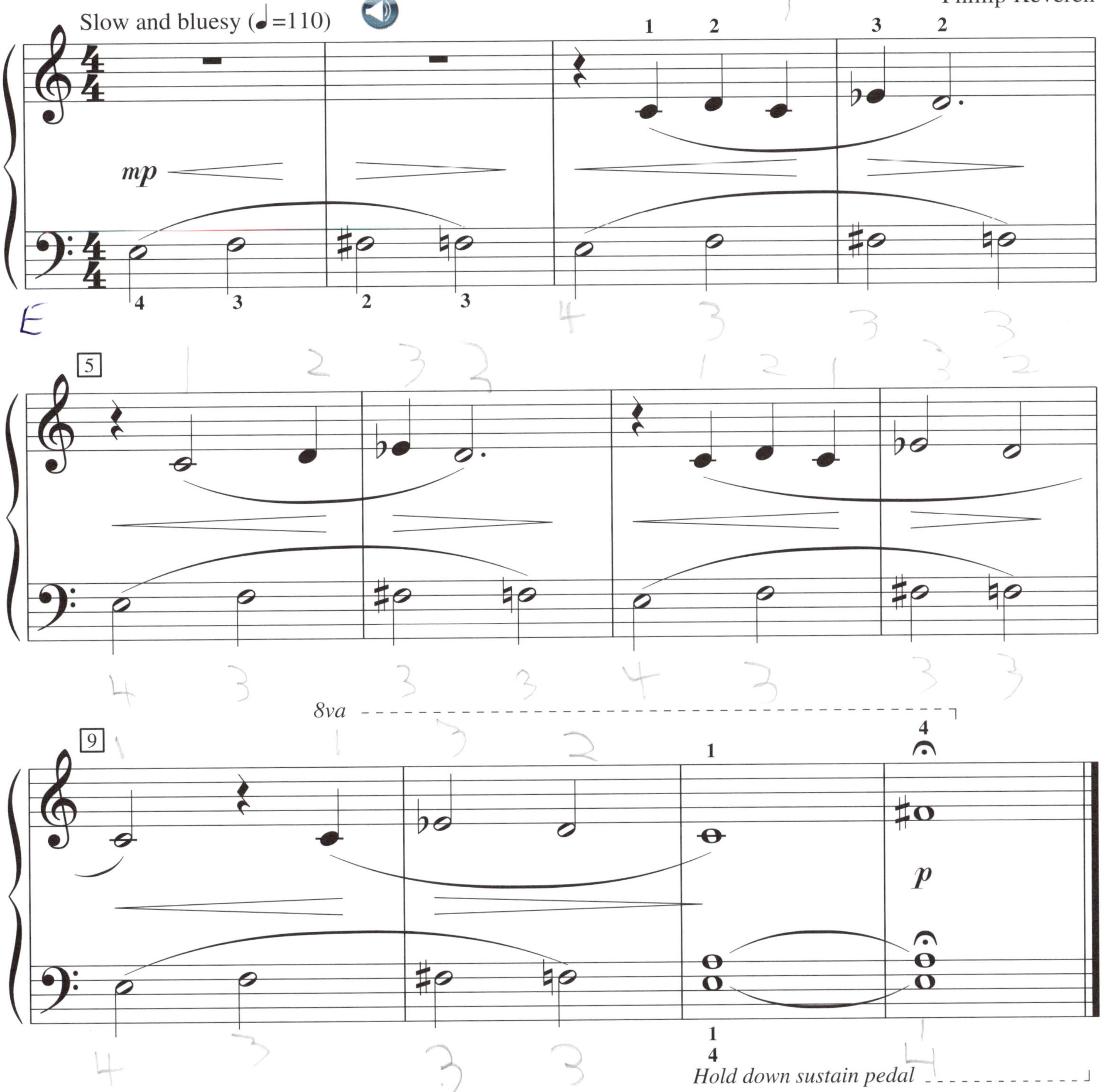

Slow and bluesy (♩=110)
mp
8va
p
Hold down sustain pedal

Serenade

Andante

Italo Taranta

Accompaniment (Student plays one octave higher than written.)

Andante (♩=145)

A sharp before a note
lasts for only one bar.

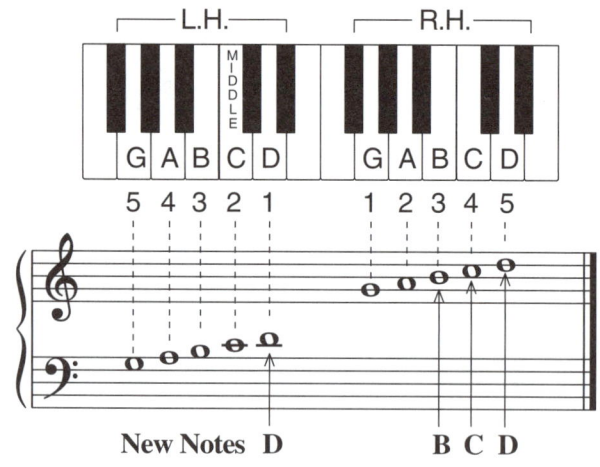

New Notes D   B C D

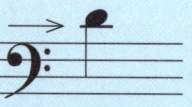

Summer Evenings

"Alouette"
Words by Barbara Kreader

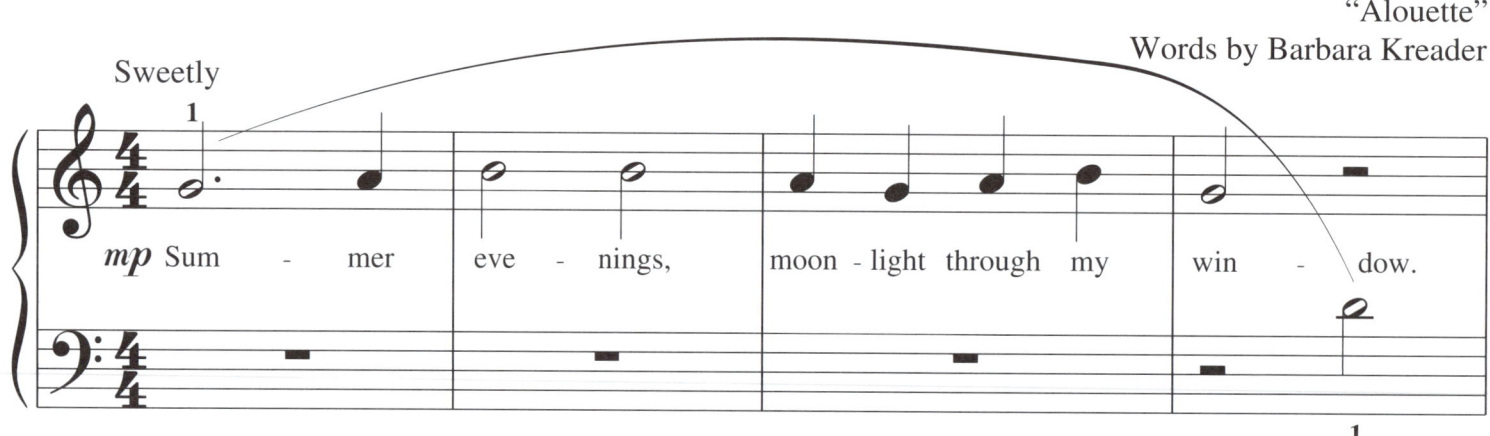

Sweetly

mp Sum - mer eve - nings, moon - light through my win - dow.

Star - light shin - ing, breez - es blow - ing sighs.

Accompaniment (Student plays one octave higher than written.)

Sweetly (♩=150)

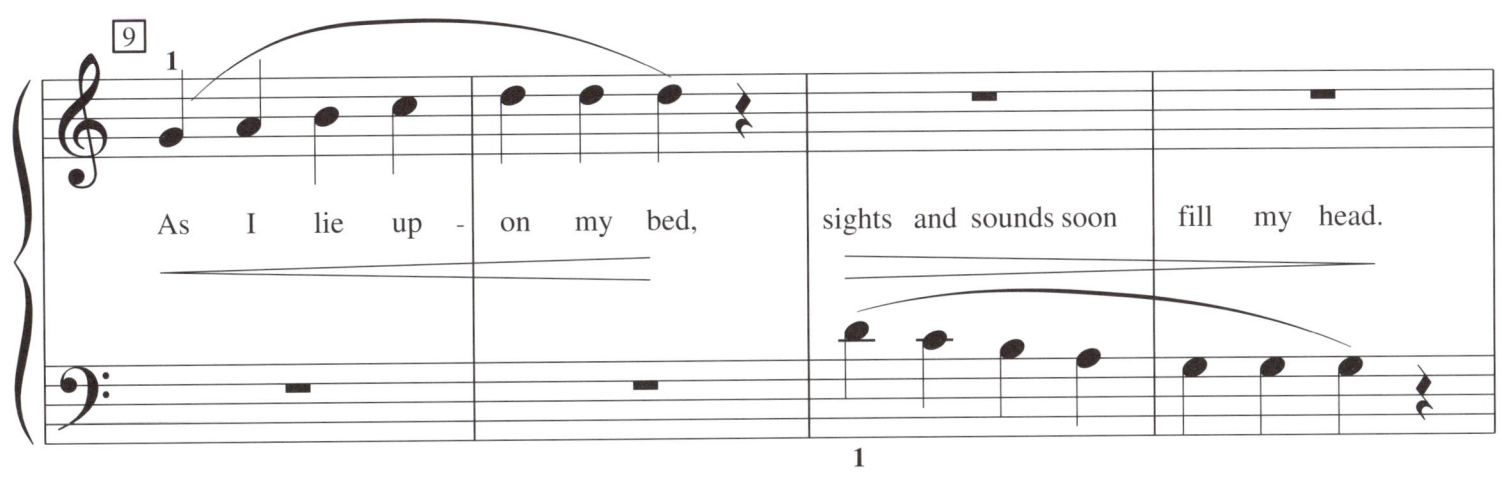

As I lie up - on my bed, sights and sounds soon fill my head.

Light - ning bugs, *mf* pass - ing cars, crick - et calls, *mp* fall - ing stars.

mf Sum - mer eve - nings warm and soft and still. *rit.*

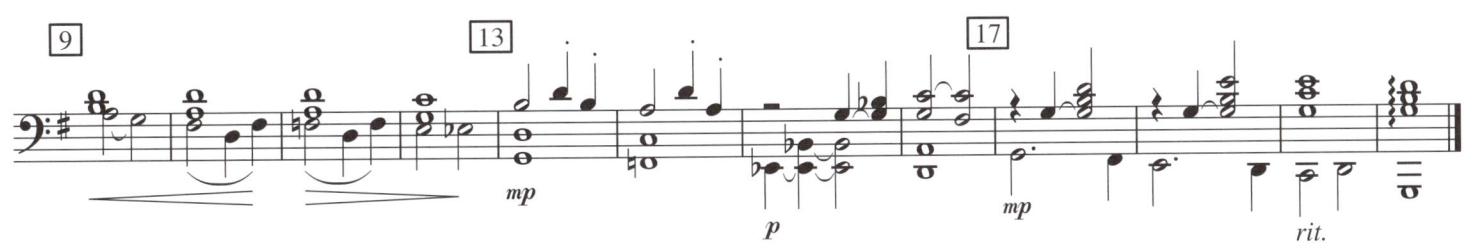

My Own Song
On G A B C D

Place both hands on G A B C D. Listen and feel the pulse as your teacher plays the accompaniment below.

With your right hand, play G A B C D. Experiment by playing D C B A G. Mix the letters any way you want and make up your own song!

With your left hand, play G A B C D. Experiment by playing D C B A G. Again, mix the letters any way you want and make up another song!

Have fun!

Accompaniment

Jazz Waltz (♩=170)

Repeat as necessary | Last time

Pop!

Bouncy (♩=200)

"Pop Goes The Weasel"

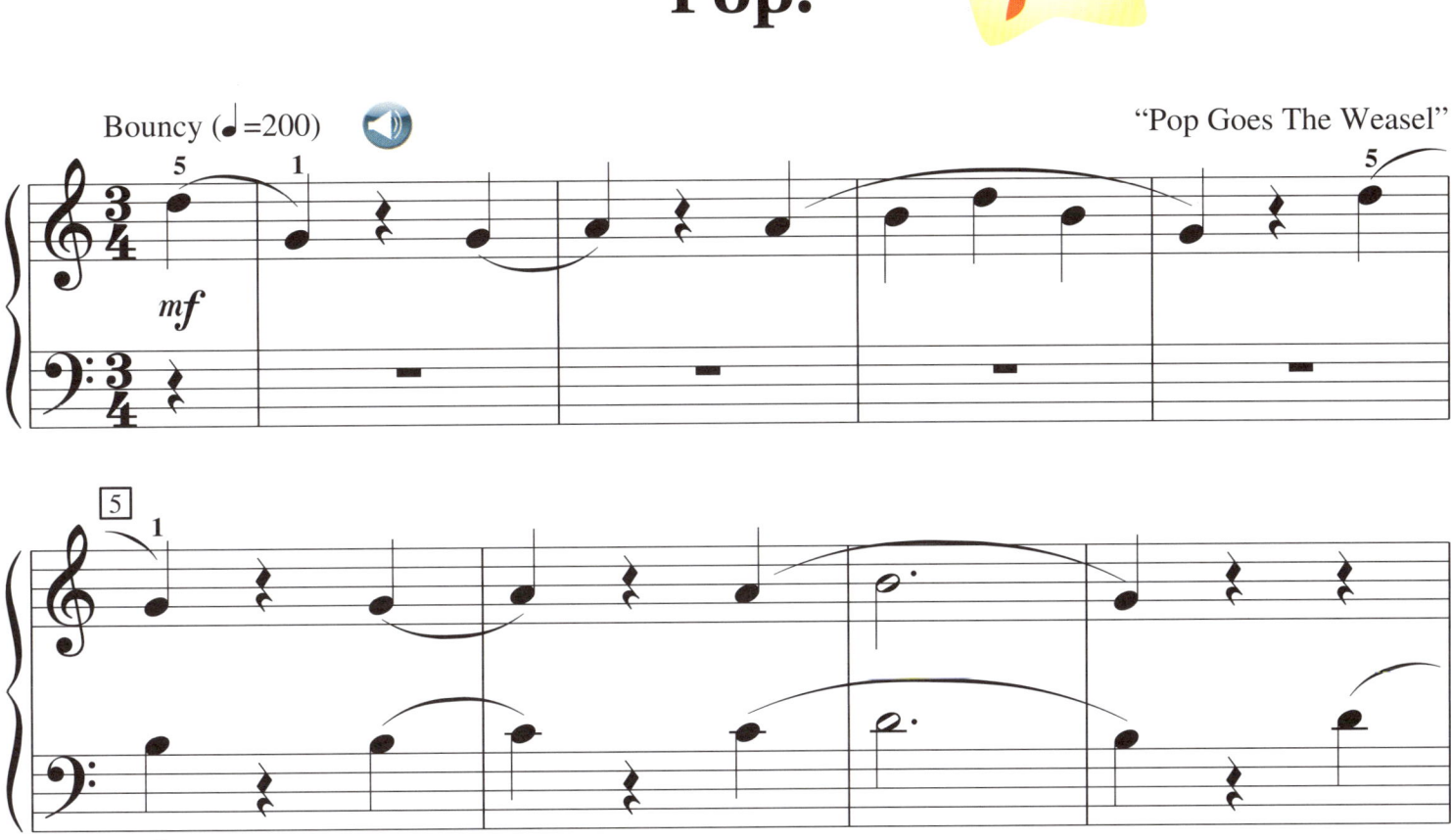

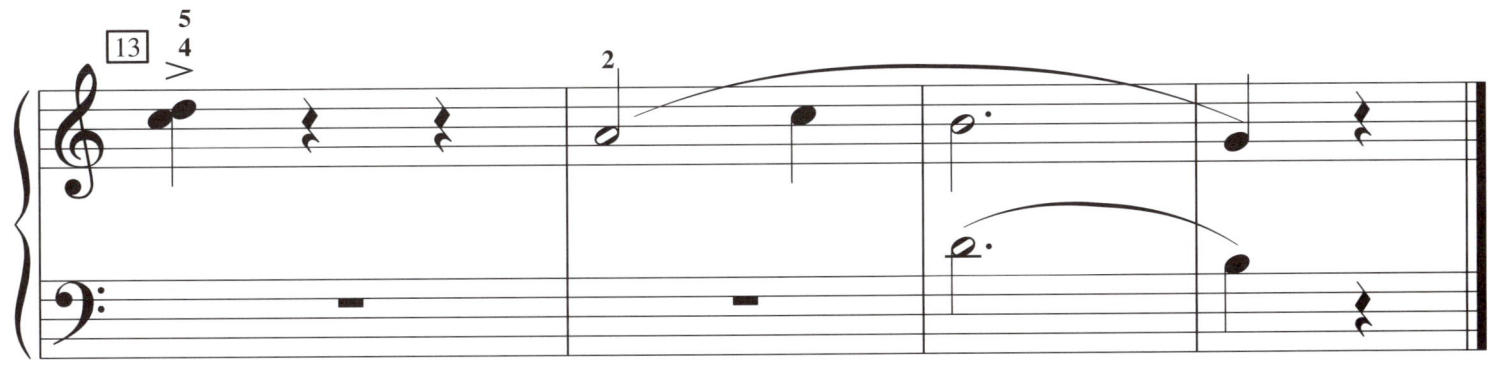

Go To Sleep

Andante

Folk Tune

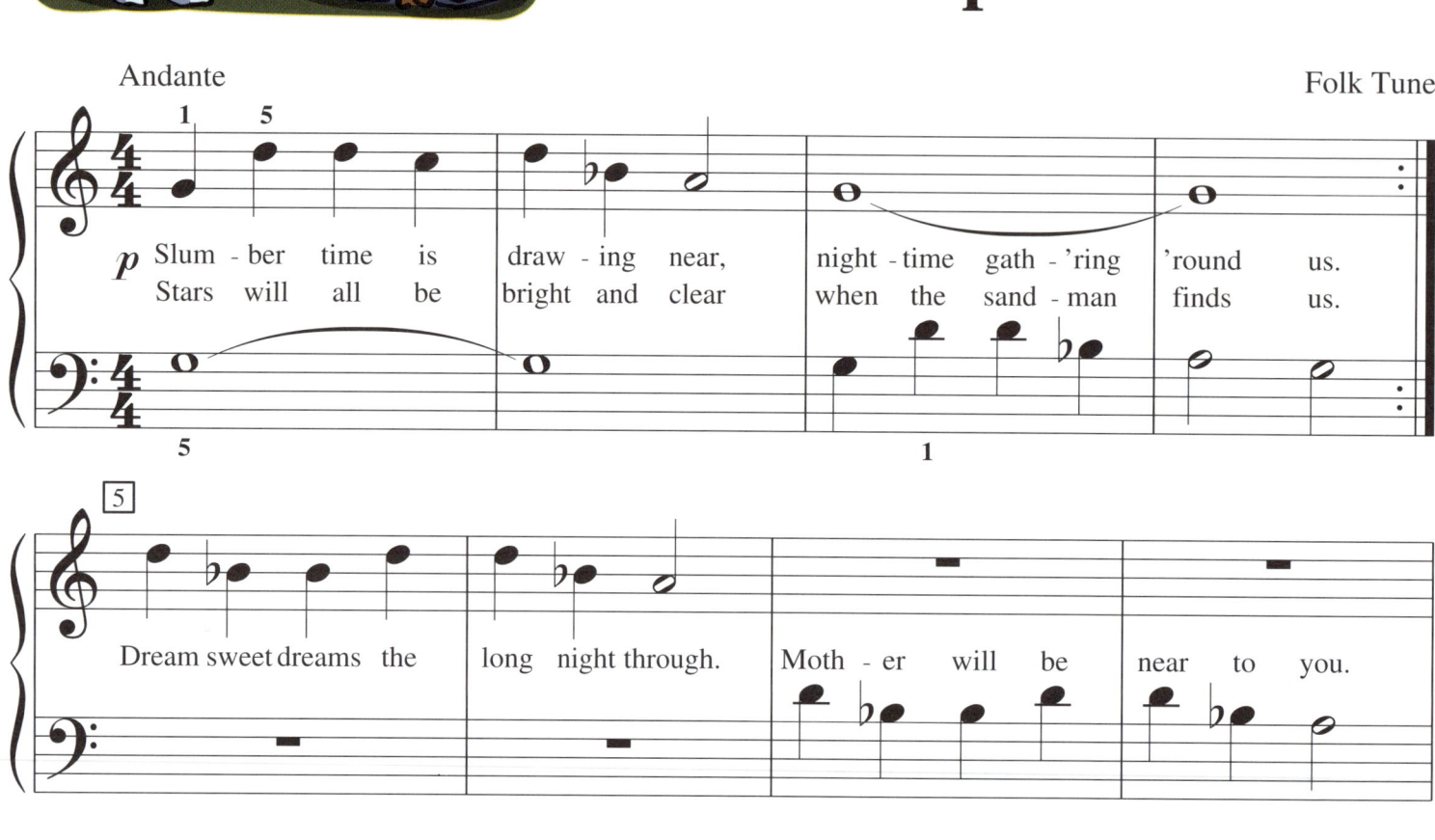

Slum - ber time is draw - ing near, night - time gath - 'ring 'round us.
Stars will all be bright and clear when the sand - man finds us.

Dream sweet dreams the long night through. Moth - er will be near to you.

Go to sleep, my dear one. Go to sleep, my dear one.

pp rit.

Accompaniment (Student plays one octave higher than written.)

Andante (♩=110)

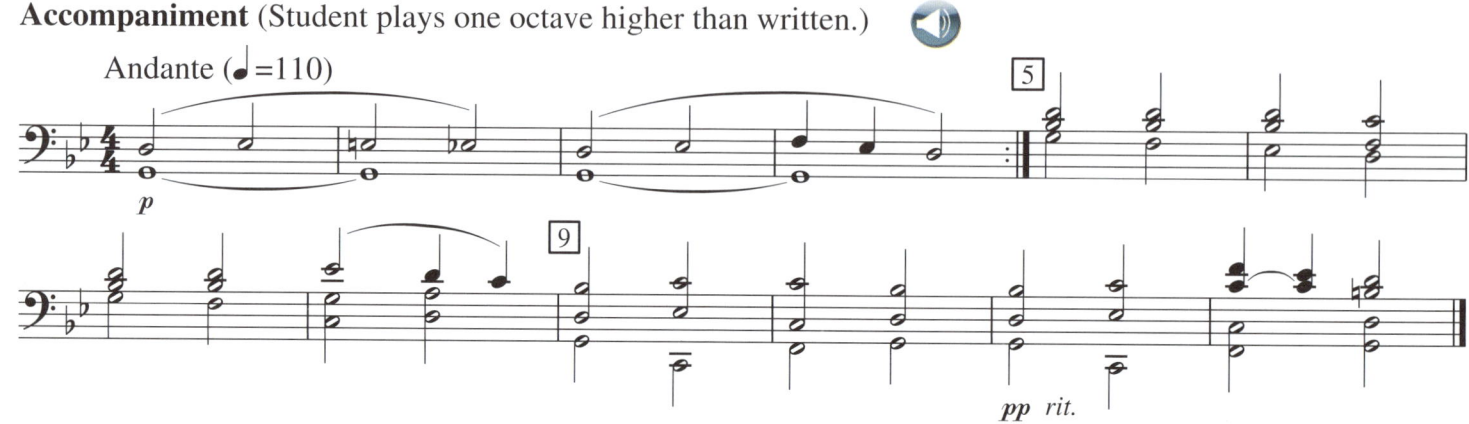

pp rit.

44

Jig

Remember,

UPBEAT

Count: "2 3   1 2 3"

Lively (♩=210)

Irish

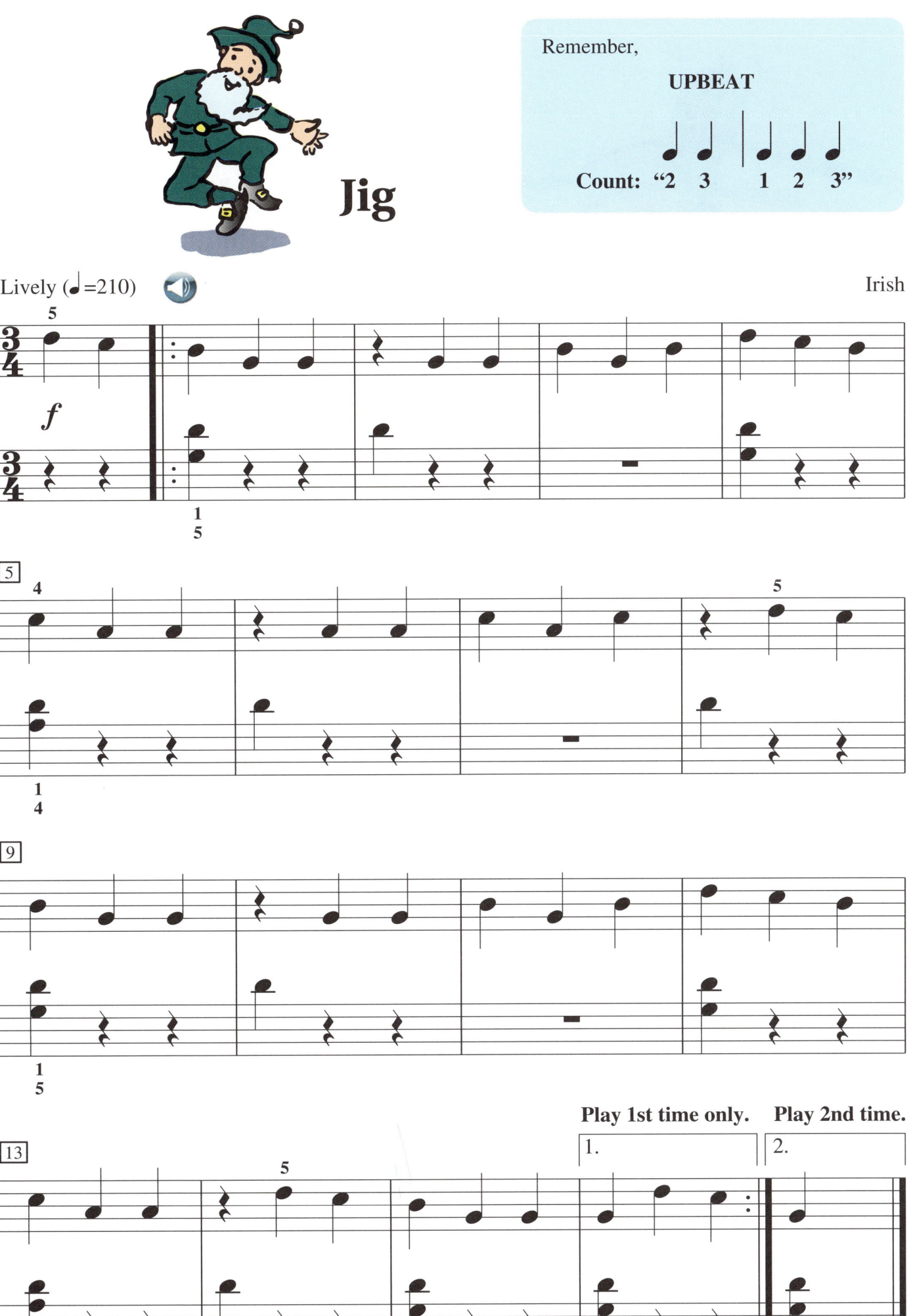

45

Go For The Gold

Stately March

Phillip Keveren

Accompaniment (Student plays one octave higher than written.)

Stately March (♩=90)

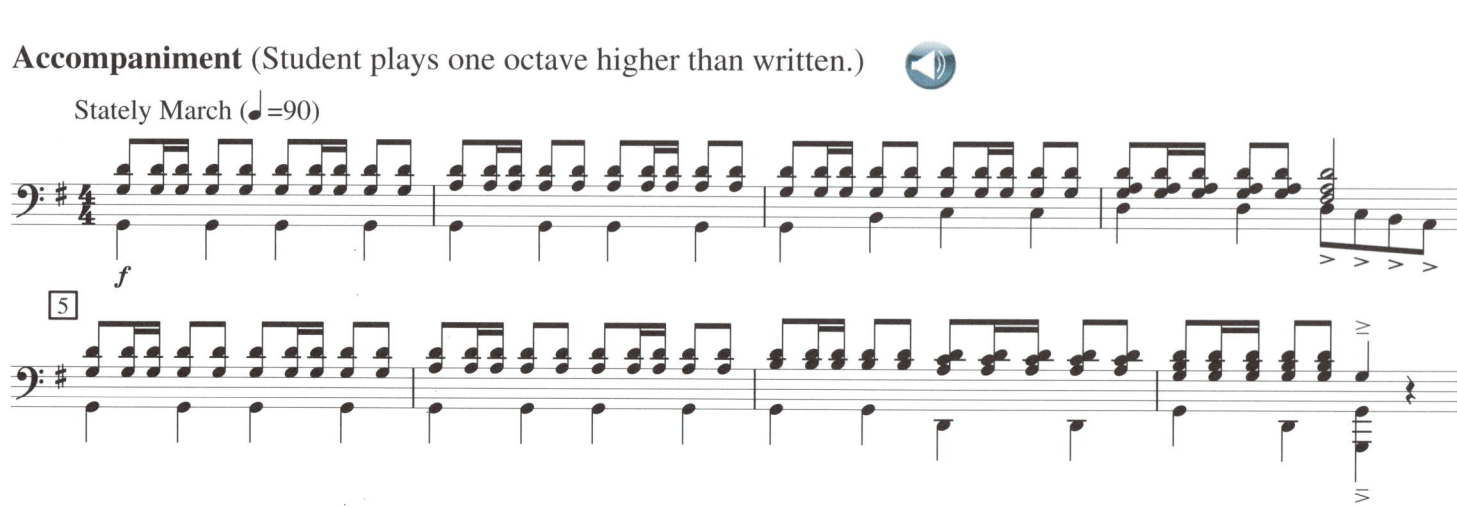

9
mf
3
2
13
1
f
1
2
17

9
mf
p
mf
p
f
13
17

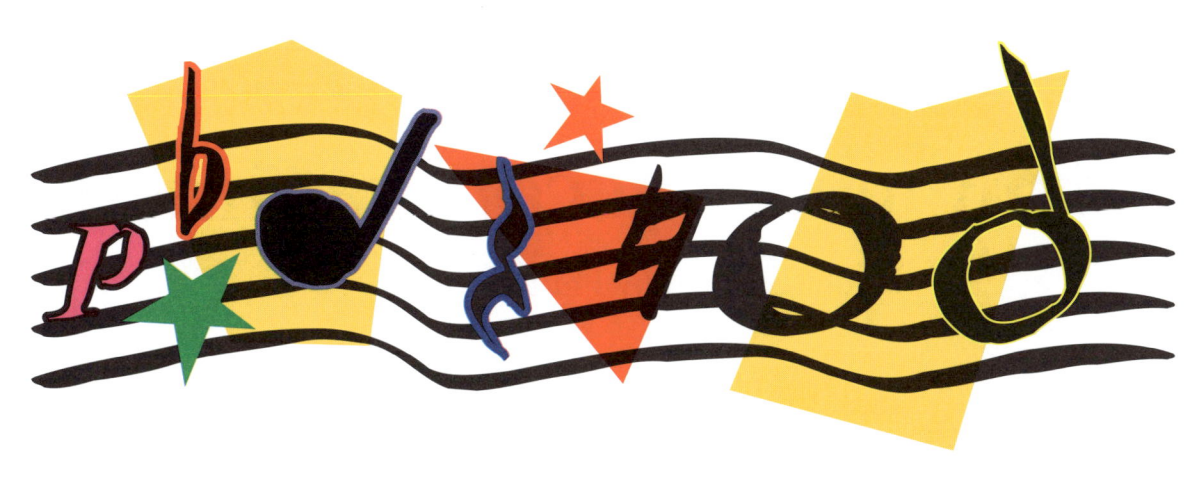

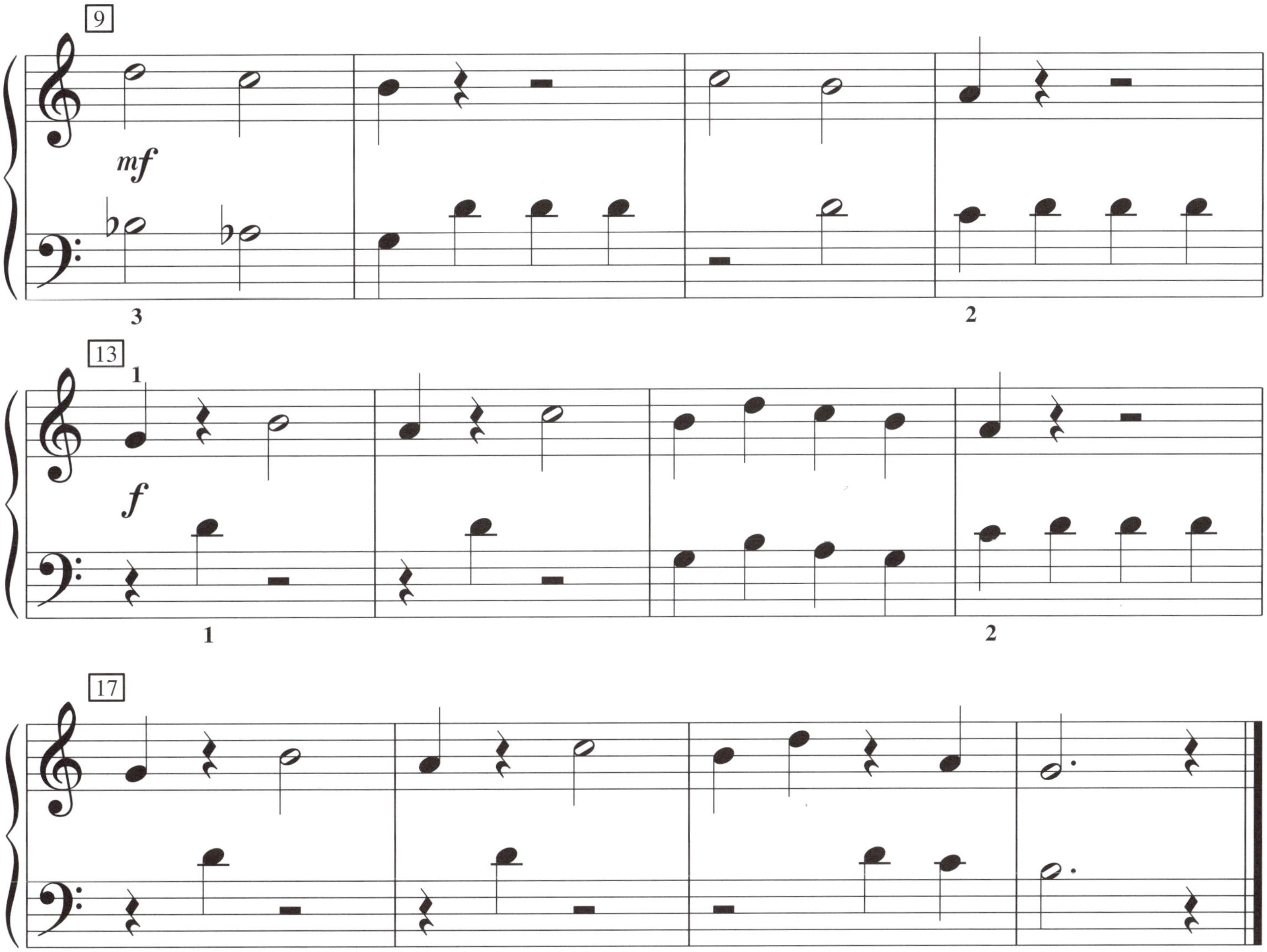

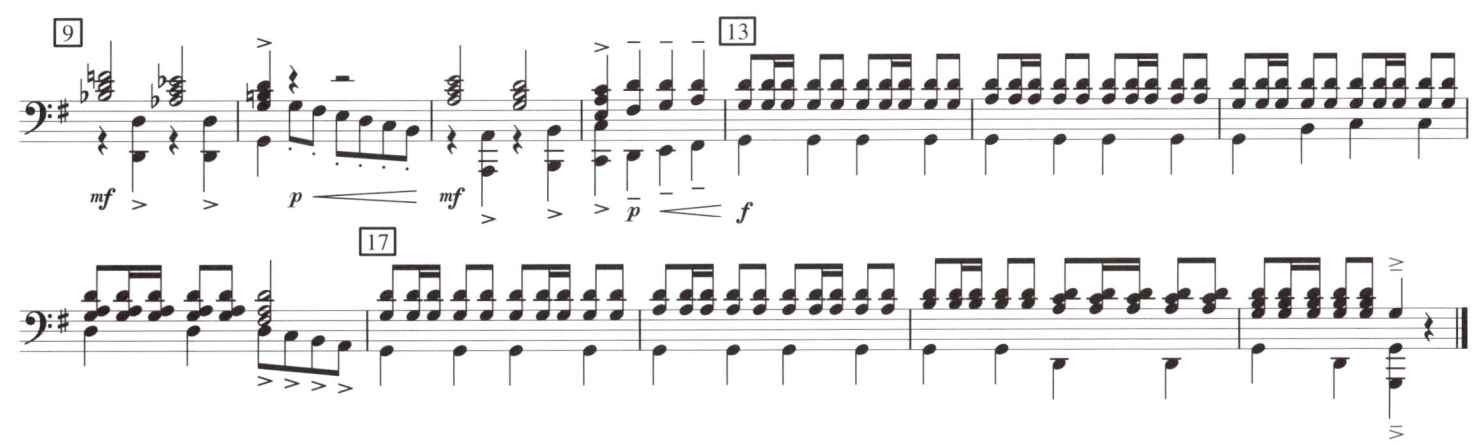

Instrumental Accompaniments

orchestrated by Phillip Keveren

Full orchestrated arrangements are included with this book and may be used for both practice and performance. There are two accompaniment tracks for each piece. The first is a practice tempo; it is slower and includes the piano melody. The second is the performance tempo—a little faster—and without the piano melody.

To access the accompanying audio and MIDI files, simply go to **www.halleonard.com/mylibrary** and enter the code found on page 1 of this book. This will grant you instant access to every file. You can download to your computer, tablet, or phone, or stream the audio live—and if your device has Flash, you can also use our *PLAYBACK+* multi-functional audio player to slow down or speed up the tempo, change keys, or set loop points. This feature is available exclusively from Hal Leonard and is included with the price of this book!

For technical support, please email **support@halleonard.com**

Audio Track List

	Page in Lesson Book	Track # with Solo *practice tempo*	Track # w/o Solo *performance tempo*		Page in Lesson Book	Track # with Solo *practice tempo*	Track # w/o Solo *performance tempo*
UNIT 1				**UNIT 4**			
Reflection	4	1	2	Little River Flowing	28	42	43
My Own Song On C D E F G	5	–	3	Quiet Thoughts	29	44	45
Ode To Joy	6	4	5	Star Quest	30	46	47
Carmen's Tune	7	6	7	A Little Latin	32	48	49
Andantino	8	8	9	Stompin'	33	50	51
Big Ben	9	10	11	First Light	34	52	53
Please, No Bees!	10	12	13	Inspector Hound	36	54	55
Clapping Song	11	14	15	Bayou Blues	37	56	57
				Serenade	38	58	59
UNIT 2							
Hoedown	12	16	17	**UNIT 5**			
Sunlight Through The Trees	13	18	19	Summer Evenings	40	60	61
Bingo	14	20	21	My Own Song On G A B C D	42	–	62
Travelling Along The Prairie	15	22	23	Pop!	43	63	64
No One To Walk With	16	24	25	Go To Sleep	44	65	66
Painted Rocking Horse	18	26	27	Jig	45	67	68
Tick Tock The Jazz Clock	20	28	29	Go For The Gold	46	69	70
UNIT 3							
Watercolors	22	30	31				
Circle Dance	23	32	33				
Basketball Bounce	24	34	35				
Allegro	25	36	37				
Great News!	26	38	39				
Brass Fanfare	27	40	41				